What Readers Say About
Slow Road Home

Like Emily Dickinson, Fred First in *Slow Road Home* notices "smallest things," things overlooked before, finds them italicized as it were, and makes them part of his memory, his diary, and now this book, vibrant with the rich sense of living things on the pages within it. Everything he sees is connected, barely visible and maybe even invisible, but clearly a part of the web of being running through space and time, linking in mystery and awe the visible world to the great spirit that animates it.

Jack Higgs, Professor Emeritus, East Tennessee State University

Fred First's *Slow Road Home*, like Thoreau's *Walden*, is an experiment in living deliberately and facing the essential facts of life. Morning after morning, First opens his eyes and remembers, using words and a naturalist's love of details to coax pattern and parable, tragedy and transcendence, out of his Floyd County meadow and creeks. His paragraphs trace the drama of the ordinary—an ordinary so rich and strange that we realize we've never been truly awake before.

Thomas Gardner, Clifford A. Cutchins Professor of English, Virginia Tech

Socrates calls us to live an examined life and Fred First heeds this call. Through these fragments from Floyd, he mends together the bits and pieces of his days to create a wholeness of a life and a book.

Jim Minick, author of Finding a Clear Path

~ Author's Note ~

I know this from my photographer's experience:
any image I take is one of a kind. Each composition in light or in words is unique. The light
will never be that color from that angle on that
exact configuration of barn, tree or wildflower
ever again.

And this: that we too often take for granted
the extraordinary senses of vision and hearing,
touch and smell that are our gifts—opportunities
given us by which we could know the familiar
beauties too often missed or dismissed in our
hurried lives.

We have so little time in the present and there
is so very much to take in and share. There are
wonders all around. From our everyday lives,
these familiar things may seem unremarkable
to us. But in these precious instants in time, if
we keep our eyes open and our hearts ready to
know it, there is nothing ordinary.

Slow Road Home

For David
& Susan
Visitors to the slow road!

Fred First
September 2006

Slow Road Home

a blue ridge
book of days

Fred First

Goose Creek Press ~ Floyd, Virginia

Published by Goose Creek Press
Floyd, Virginia

Copyright © 2006 by Fred First

Images and book design
by Fred First

For information, email gckpress@gmail.com

or go to goosecreekpress.com

ISBN: 0-9779395-0-2

ISBN-13: 9-780977-939503

SAN: 8 5 0 – 6 7 4 4

Acknowledgements

I confess that I have most often thumbed right past this kind of page in the past. I doubt I ever will again, now that I understand the collaboration involved. It truly takes a village to birth a book, and to those good citizens, I owe a debt of gratitude.

For the hope that there could be a book in all the words from mornings on Goose Creek, I owe Dr. Jack Higgs, who had faith when I had only doubt. Dr. Tom Gardner contributed his ability to see patterns and helped me to find order in the apparent chaos, and persisted and encouraged until the job was done.

To the readers of Fragments from Floyd: thank you for giving me a sense of audience; for your voices and your ears. I trust that the book carries you a step closer to feeling like you have been here for that front porch visit many of us have hoped some day to have.

Thanks to my voluntary editors, reviewers and technical advisors who gave me feedback from the final drafts and others who nudged me up the learning curve in the book-making arts. Mary Beth Bower at Edwards Brothers was a stalwart from the very start, before and even after she learned how very many questions one man can ask.

This book required a span of time when there were no returns for investment. Wife, Ann, gave her blessing for me to work from home, learn from this place, and write about it. This was a gift, and this book a fruit of those mornings alone that she gave me.

Contents

Preface

Where Does This Road Go?

When it's time, a man walks away from his job—and possibly, from his profession. When he does, he leaves his identity, his moorings and his maps. He abandons landmarks that have told him where he has belonged in the world, and may find at first that he doesn't know where he belongs in the world apart from his work.

It was 1987 when we left the little blue Wythe County farmhouse, our first country home with the old apple orchard in the yard; a home where our son was born and learned to fly and our daughter had a horse and a secret club house hidden in the hay bales of the barn loft. We drove south, leaving behind twelve years of belonging in Virginia. We left a place we loved and were secure, so that I could change careers from teaching biology to practicing physical therapy and live happily ever after.

When Ann and I finally returned to Virginia in 1997, I had the satisfaction of having helped patients in clinics in three states. But over the years in healthcare, there grew to be more management and senseless paperwork, and less satisfaction. I suppose I could make a long list of the reasons I left my job that day. And there are good reasons that I could not have told you then. "The heart has reasons that reason does not know" and this time, at fifty four, to my surprise, I chose to follow my heart.

I cleared my office drawers and loaded boxes of files into my truck at the clinic that Friday in May, 2002, with an unsettling but strangely liberating realization that I may never return to physical therapy again. For the first time since the mid-seventies, when Ann and I pulled the U-Haul from Alabama to our new home in Virginia with such naïve high hopes, I had no Plan B. Monday came, I stayed home.

"Take your time" Ann said. "See what happens." I decided not to look for another job or explore the possibilities of a third career right away. But as far as I could see into the months ahead, the calendar was an empty hole in time. The days held the terror of uncertainty and the exhilaration of freedom. But freedom without purpose can be a kind of bondage. What was I meant to do if not what I'd always done? The vision would come. It always had. Where was my faith?

Every morning that first month in my ambivalent sabbatical, I watched the tail lights of Ann's car disappearing through the pines as she left for work, flickering past the silhouettes of trees, red against black, up and out of sight and sound. She was the provider now. And what had I become—the custodian, the gardener, a house-sitting tenant on my own land?

I stood there at the open door with my coffee in the dark with a day ahead of me—a day that would have been a treasure during thirty years of work when a morning-to-evening just for me was rare, and home only a place to spend the nights and weekends. And now, I had the whole day alone here—a place we thought we would grow to know well some day—after we retired, perhaps. Ann had given it a name: Here's Home, our place in the country. I could walk the place from dawn until dusk and not see the same tree twice. I might follow along the ridges, or wade in Goose Creek or along the one that no map had thought worthy of a name, that I called Nameless Creek. And in those places, I would spend my day in utter quiet.

But when this unplanned day ended, I might have no new purpose, no point to move toward, no *reason to be*. When she came home tired and drained at the end of the day, what was I to tell her that I had done with my time alone? What did I do *for a living* now, in this uncharted space of days, weeks, maybe longer? It was a question not casually asked.

The answer came over the summer, through uneven months of anguish and hope. And it seemed so impractical, so merely poetic and delusional that when I finally knew, I was reluctant to tell it. But here it was: my work would be in getting to know my part here at home—a home where I did not fully belong those mornings as the valley took shape and its textures appeared softly in the first sun of dawn, flaming red against the barn roof. For the days ahead, my goal each foggy morning and everynight under the stars would be to find wonder and meaning in whatever kind of light the days or nights would bring.

Nothing would be ignored, no thing trivial: not the wind or the woods; not the rain or the water underground or the creeks. The garden, the forest, the sounds of summer, the wonders of imagination, the familiar unnamed smells of the seasons—all of these common elements just beyond the front steps would be objects of curiosity and importance.

I revisited stories from memories past and found them new in each new day's reflection from some part of our valley. Alone in my own time and space, I settled here, grounding myself in my own history and in the present moment. I was both author and subject of a very personal narrative. It seemed a story worth telling if for no one else but me, and a story that only I could tell. And this was the time that had been set aside for me to do it. This would be my work.

I stopped wearing my watch; there were no schedules or deadlines. Rhythms changed from the hurry-sick pace of corporate imperative to the natural cycles of change in each hour and day, days on end. I spent time—as much as I needed—sitting still on the ridge, walking by the creek, leaning on my rake in the garden. In the slowness, in the stillness, words and images came, not every morning but most—a kind of manna I had never known. From those fragments of the ordinary, a chronicle of the seasons of the Blue Ridge took shape here—one place in all the world we seemed destined to find, and I was determined now to know.

I began to write every day, keeping a kind of field note-book—for myself, and as it turns out, for a small audience of readers who found me here and followed my account of life on Goose Creek by way of a weblog that I called *Fragments from Floyd*. There, I recorded whatever came to mind or to heart, gathering images, making pages for our book of days. It would become a guidebook to bring back the sound of wind in winter and the smell of pasture grass in moonlight; to remember the way it feels to watch the first fire of autumn in the stove or bring in the harvest from the garden; to lose a dog too soon, or gain the love of his successor at the edge of the creek.

Patterns form that we cannot see when we stand too close to the moments that make them. In what follows, I've drawn out selections from many mornings of writing, and grouped them in such a way that the shape of where I've been, where I live and what I've done for a living over the past three years begins to emerge.

I thought I was completely at sea as I was writing through that first perplexing year, June 2002 through July 2003. Looking back at that period as I sorted through those entries, pattern and purpose appeared. I could see my focus changing, as if I had used three different lenses to discover the seasonal rhythms of that year.

"Still and Still Moving" is like a microscope lens for looking in, for following the senses carefully, for dis-covering meaning in the fine details of everyday things. "Leaf, Feather and Fur" focuses wide-angle on nature and the creatures and landforms that share this valley with me. And "Roads Remembered" turns the telescope backwards on those people and places that are the fixed mountain peaks of my past, orienting my map along the road to the present.

The pieces in the second section of vignettes, "Rooted, Grounded, Found" are also arranged by the month in which each piece was written, though they span from Summer 2003 to Fall 2005. The lens is the full focus of one man's vision, and they are more personal, ranging from the sublimity of falling snow to the absurdities of married life. I think of them as a celebration of the beautiful ordinary, in which I am finally at home.

Part One:
Still, and Still Moving

Stranger in a Strange Land

I don't have a job to go to and I don't have a plan for what comes next. And yet, somehow, I am not as anxious about this as I would have thought I'd be.

But I do feel guilty—as if I had skipped school. I pull back behind the curtains when the few cars go by the house, lest their drivers, our neighbors, see that I'm not at work on a weekday. I tell myself to relax and enjoy being here while I can. This is not house arrest. It is not punishment. It is an odd kind of time apart from work that might become more like an unplanned vacation be-tween jobs—a strange vacation, I'll grant you—just me here all day, every day. The place seems unfamiliar, like a bed-and-breakfast, somewhere I've spent many nights but not so many days. Maybe the next few weeks will be a sort of spiritual retreat, one novitiate and one big black dog in eighty acres of quiet sanctuary.

My work for now is living fully in this alien world, moving in a smaller orbit. This is a world not made or managed by man—a natural world of cold creeks inhabited by mayapples and scarlet tanagers. This is a planet where I am learning to smell the changes as the season unfolds, taste the first cup of coffee under stars before the sun comes up over the ridge, and enjoy the comfort and companionship of the pup—blessings that persist even while some things have come undone, for a while.

So here I am all at once, thrown into this brier patch, a beautiful place to be tossed, though I would not have chosen to get here this way. I still feel like a stranger in my own country, but less so than last month. Three months from now, will I be more content with my lot? Will I be by then so immersed in this place that I look like it, become invisible against it, evolving, camouflaged and part of the landscape myself? Will I become lost here, or found?

Summer Lightning

It is late, and I am last to bed, past the usual time. I step out onto the front porch into the cool, sweet air of early June, and sit on the top step quietly as if not to disturb the wildlife, whose nocturnal day I am entering.

The pasture grasses just beyond the maples are in full flower and their pollen smells like midnight bread baking, while Goose Creek sends up wafts of spearmint, wet mud and turbulence.

My eyes soon learn to see in darkness and I am aware of soundless flashes of summer lightning, and stars overhead. My night vision comes and goes with each flash and pause and flash. Rising from the dark field on the fragrance of grasses are tens of thousands of lightning bugs. Put them in a jar, shake and see them illumined with the cold translucence of memory. They pulse and rise above the field in counterpoint to the tempo of the clouds, signaling ancient syllables that we could understand, if we were more often still, less hurried, and more at home in our own pastures.

Gravity pulls me down and I lie on my back, on cool stone horizontal, before a mock-infinity of space, wondering what is my place in this world of men and of words? Do I deserve to be so blessed among Earth's teeming humanity? What must I do in the warmth of this gentle epiphany that is revealed to me tonight and how should I then live? Maybe I will try to find the words in the morning, after the house is quiet again and the fireflies have gone to bed and the world smells of heat and ozone and toast.

What I Do I Do For a Living

"So, what do you do?" a stranger asks. For him, it's just polite conversation. But this question makes me break out in a cold sweat. What am I supposed to say to him? Am I a gentleman farmer now; a domestic engineer; a stay-at-home husband? Am I a former teacher, former physical therapist, former income earner? I'm not sure if I'm between jobs, or out to pasture, or starting over in a new career that I can't name. I do know that when I wake up in the morning and groggily project my mind forward into the day ahead, it's not the biology classroom or lab where I see myself and it's definitely not a day in the clinic full of patients in pain.

Truth is, the first thing that comes to mind in the morning, before my eyes are open and my feet hit the floor, are the things I want to say and images I want to show to my weblog readers. I've come to think about *Fragments from Floyd* as my work, what I do with my day, what I look forward to—to simply write out the days as they come. I feel no burning urgency to go back to healthcare just for the paycheck. For a while, with some frugal belt tightening, we can meet our bills on one salary. But it is her salary, not mine and hers, as it has been for more than thirty years. I'm non-productive now, a parasite, and no matter how I turn it in my mind, that shakes up my male ego more than a little.

Our good friend Lynn died suddenly in her sleep last month at forty-five. She left projects that she will never finish. She had visions of things she would someday do that now will be left undone forever. She died one ordinary day in the midst of a busy life. Maybe she expected the end. Maybe she knew her treasure wasn't in making more money. When she left us, I feel sure that she was doing with her life what she would have done, had she known. Months before, she left a lucrative business so she could create, so she could invest her energies in the things she loved. Her death has come just when my life was changing, just when I've been given this opportunity to dig for treasure in a different place.

I am digging, and sometimes finding, even when I'm only working in the garden or bringing in the wood. Maybe this is what I *do for a living* now. I put away scraps from the everyday, collect odd bits of experience and memory—strings of adjectives, strong verbs, the small revelations or perplexities I discover under rocks while exploring the creek bank. I keep curiosities that make me smile—a nice phrase here, an alliterative couplet there, or some odd voice I hear in the wind or water. I once threw away such foolish things. Now I save them all. My journal is a junk drawer—a place to save the parts I might one day need for a paragraph. I dig into the jumbled springs and strings, wires and washers and pull out the piece I want, to tie up a sentence. I don't throw away scraps of language anymore. I am a collector of fragments from these days on Nameless Creek.

Far From it All: Solitude

While the garden endures autumn's final indignities, we eat the last of the fresh chard, Chinese cabbage and kale. The canning shelves downstairs are heavy with Mason jars shimmering in yellows, greens and reds. The success of the garden this year has been a godsend. It has given me something to hold in my hands—a gratuity for the yardman, the caretaker, the gardener and security force at Here's Home. Produce is my paycheck.

We give up a few minutes of daylight each day. The leaning corn browns and withers. Starlings gather and fret in the trees along the creek. Monarchs should be passing through soon while the wooly worms look for winter shelter, always across the road. For the past months, garden plants have been like children who needed my care. Now they are going away for another year, and I will be left with empty hours. That little plot of earth has drawn me out of doors since May. Working under the sky has lifted my spirits when I grew discouraged. Now I think about the coming months of being here alone—just me and Buster, the black velvet dog—housebound during the short, dark days of winter. But I have been alone before.

Dry Wells

We turned on the floor fan for the first time last night as we were going to bed, to keep the still, humid air stirred up a little. I woke up a few hours later, bothered by the noise of the whirring blades. I'd much rather hear the outside sounds coming through the open window—a trilling toad, a whippoorwill, a screech owl over by the barn. I switched off the fan, and stepped out onto the porch into the tepid night before getting back to my dreams.

The earth lay silver and still. High clouds pulled past the face of the moon like a silk scarf, flooding the valley with pulses of lavender light. The barred owl's who-cooks-for-you, the other night so close to the house, called from farther down the pasture, near the crook in the ridge where the creek disappears up the canyon of leaning oaks and white pines. Crickets and katydids were in full evening voice, sine-waves rising, falling, their chorus mesmerizing in its repetitiveness, mantra-like and reassuring.

But something was lacking, and I did not at first grasp what it was. A layer in this night chorus was missing from its accustomed place, and I stood there in the dark with an unsettling emptiness.

Then I knew: the creeks were silent. For the first time since we've known nights here, Goose Creek and Nameless Creek that converge outside our bedroom window were not the dominant background of sound. That turbulent chatter has been so always-present, we have taken it for granted until now. Tonight, an entire section of our orchestra was mute, the silence itself a kind of jarring noise.

Wells across our region are drying up from the three-year drought. And it is not just the wells that are drying but the very source—the vast waters in bedrock where most of the drinkable water on Earth is found. When this source goes dry, it takes years, maybe decades to replenish. Some wells and springs will never come back after a sustained drought like this, leaving dark caves and crevices silent and dry far beneath our feet—places that have been wet with liquid sounds since these mountains were born.

Showers of Blessing

I leaned against the garden fence this morning, holding my hat in my hand as if I was standing in a cemetery, bereft. The corn listed at odd angles. Its brown leaves were curled and brittle, rustling like a November scarecrow in the parched winds of mid-August. Half-ripe Hubbard squash lay hidden by limp and drooping leaves, the fruits not ripe enough to pick but so close to ready that it seemed an awful waste to pull them from the dust. The vines would die back in another day or two of the drought.

South of us, thick gray clouds have been sagging since mid-morning, but I've learned that they can't be trusted. I watch the signs like an ancient shaman examining bird bones, looking for some portent of future rain. Its falling on the horizon now is illusion, a mirage that the weathermen call virga: an unfulfilled promise. We see its gray streaks streaming from the clouds beyond the barn, but not a drop reaches the ground before it vanishes into vapor. It has been so long since the last drops fell that when they come—if they come—they will be a liquid miracle, a holy gift, the ordinary become extraordinary for its scarcity.

Later in the morning, they did come: three large, fat drops kersplatted on the walk outside the porch door. But God was not in the cloud, and those few drops were followed by nothing but a high, hot wind. Somewhere overhead, it was raining while dust devils danced along the edges of my garden, taunting and cruel. Three drops. Better none at all.

I lay down shirtless on the stone walkway outside the back door and watched a dry wind draw exaggerated demons and cherubs in shades of slate and pewter; but a gray, flat and featureless rain cloud would have been the most angelic and beautiful vision of all. I barely noticed the commotion rushing up our valley from the south. Another dry wind, I thought, as the warmth from the stone walkway sedated me into a dehydrated daydreaming torpor.

Then, sudden, sustained and smelling of dust and ozone, the blessed rain came. It swept in sheets up the valley, toward the house, passing over me where I lay—supine and supplicant in baptism. It is raining still.

This afternoon, we have walked in it, waded in it, rejoiced in it. How frail we are in that the cellular seas inside us, plant and animal alike, are filled by rains and rivers that we do not own and cannot invoke by word or law. We live on a Water Planet, but it is all too easy to think of this miraculous liquid as ordinary. I hope that I never will again, or complain about it when it comes once more in glorious excess.

Heart of Darkness

How wonderfully still it is this early morning before dawn. The rush of the creek, the sound of a distant screech owl, my own breathing—everything there is to hear in the dark. The pasture is visible only in the way that its blackness is somehow different from the black of the forested ridges. And up above and all around me, as my eyes adjust to the absence of light, is light—ancient, otherworldly, heavenly. My old friends, the constellations, like the seasonal flowers and garden vegetables, are right on time to mark the march of days into one more autumn.

The procession of the constellations back to their winter posts has begun. The Summer Triangle still appears overhead, but later to rise each night, and Aquila the Eagle and Cygnus the Swan are migrating too, as are their earthly feathered kin this season. It is dark enough to see the Northern Coal Sack, that immense cloud of light-absorbing dust that cloaks a mere billion lights of the Milky Way. Here is darkness upon darkness that few city dwellers ever see.

I haven't spent as much time under the dark night sky as I used to. Maybe we would be the better for it if we spent more time out of doors at night, so the stars could speak to us of eternity and the darkness make us whole again.

Of Moderation, Mice and Men

I have given my middle-aged self a stern lecture about the need to undertake hard physical work in a more risk-aware way this year. Gathering firewood I consider strenuous physical labor and it seems I hold this opinion more strongly as each wood-burning year passes. What I once was able to do for endless hours in the wood lot, I limit myself now to no more than twenty minutes at a time. Then, I switch to another part of the task, giving different sets of muscles and joints a chance to rest. This is what therapists call "task rotation." I should listen to my own best therapy advice. So this morning's wood gathering was more ceremonial than practical. The dog and I went through the motions to ease our cycles back into the rhythm of early winter, even if we might not bring home a cord of wood, cut and neatly stacked.

And sure enough when it was all said and done, we didn't bring home much wood. But it was high times together, just us two guys—and between the two of us, I think Buster had the better day. He is convinced that the whole process of wood gathering is, after all, about him. Every log turned is for the purpose of exposing a mouse nest or a mole's tunnel. He can barely wait for me to lift each piece off the ground until he begins digging furiously in just that spot. He is, after all, a champion mouser.

In the dog-belly-high pasture grass, he sniffs them out, and finding the scent, freezes in a classic point, with one paw raised, leaning forward, quivering. Then suddenly he springs like Tigger, leaping vertically with his paws pulled tight against his broad chest until at the last instant, he sticks his landing, front feet hard into the prey, real or imagined. You can tell he thinks himself terrible and fierce, and very wolf-like. You see, I have told him about Farley Mowat discovering that wolves feed heavily on mice; since then, his canine confidence has bordered on unrestrained lupine arrogance.

I sectioned up a spalted maple log I had been saving for my friend Lynn, who wanted to use the lumber for furniture making. But the log had "gone to the bad" after two years on the ground under the gnarled old apple tree by the creek, and Lynn left us unexpectedly with a vast wealth of chestnut and walnut stored up for projects she will never start now. So, we did our work mindfully, Buster and I, sawing up that old maple for the winter ahead.

This wood will heat me twice, maybe more, as wood cutting is said to do. It warmed me as we worked to think of the lives of my friend and the fallen maple and the standing wizard of an apple tree. I gave thanks that, at least in short bursts, hard work still warms me, too, and feels mighty good on a late September early morning, until the sun comes over the ridge, and the sweatshirt and cap come off. Those tough chunks of maple that we brought to the house today will heat me again, come December, when we will stay indoors much of the time, and I will read to Buster more inspiring tales of northern adventure.

Warming to Winter

Ann, the dog, and I took our walk early this morning. With the shortening days, the sky was coal mine dark save for the waning light of a gibbous moon. Shadows of the ridgetop forest fingered across the western half of the valley pasture. Moonlight and shadow set worlds apart—the worlds of silver-gray moon-lightness and of deep cobalt darkness, a diorama in monochrome.

In the dew, leaf and bough glistened and winked as we walked wordlessly. But moonlight was not the only light, after all. Tiny glow worms made their own from deep in the lifeless grasses, the insect's glow just perceptibly amber, the dewdrops crystal-silver with moonglow. We watched our breath rise in a vapor ahead of us. Winter was very near.

Gossamer Days

It might have been a heavenly invasion I saw on that calm, late-September day as I walked up toward the house from the woods. As it dropped just below the top of the tulip poplars, the sun shone brilliantly in the dry air of early autumn. With my eyes barely in the shadow of the dense foliage, beyond the treetop I could see dozens of dazzling specks suspended in the sun's rays. They might have been slowly westward-moving daytime satellites, or very high-flying reconnaissance aircraft. They might not have been from this world at all.

This unexpected visitation was unsettling, and I watched uncertain what it was that I was seeing. Then, a speck with a tail floated by! And another, with an even longer undulating silver thread streaming behind the mote of light, a tail that appeared to be of fantastic length. The filament was shining from within — a floating fiber-optic strand visible a quarter mile away. The webs came in waves, moving passively in the currents of an invisible sea. Flying things with silver wings, beetles perhaps, swam frantically against the current but all were swept along westward and out of view.

The silent procession continued for a short while, until the sun's setting toward the horizon by a few degrees shut out the lights of the shining wings and webs. There was no one but the dog to tell of this amazing thing, this epiphany that I had received most accidentally, unsought and unexpected. Wondering how universal my private vision of the floating spiders might be, I found what is called the "Spider Letter" written by a twelve year old Jonathan Edwards to a judge, a friend of his father's, in 1723. It was as if young Jonathan had been peering over my shoulder, as he described precisely what I had seen:

> In a very calm and serene day in the aforementioned time of year [late August to late September] standing at some distance between the end of a house or some other opaque body, so as just to hide the disk of the sun and keep off his dazzling rays, and looking along close by the side of it, I have seen vast multitudes of little shining webs and glistening strings, brightly reflecting the sunbeams, and some of them of a great length, and at such a height that one would think that they were tacked to the vault of the heavens . . . making a very pleasing as well as surprising appearance. It is wonderful at what a distance these webs may plainly be seen in such a position to the sunbeams; some at a great distance appear several thousands of times as big as they ought. . .There appears at the end of these webs spiders sailing in the air with them, doubtless with an abundance of pleasure, though not so much as I have beheld them and shewd them to others. And since I have seen these things I have been very conversant with spiders.

A revelation of radiant webs like prayers floating unseen above my head for fifty autumns has made me forever-more conversant with floating spiders. Perhaps they are angels. What wonders hide beneath my boots or hover in air just above my skin, I cannot imagine. Look up. Miracles must be everywhere.

Fortress of Solitude: October Rain

From the front porch this morning, it would be hard to tell if any remaining fall song birds are singing. The *drip drip plunk* on the metal roof, the soft hiss of tiny drops as they fall, and the blessed gush of a creek from bank to bank dominate the audiosphere. We've more water headed toward the Atlantic today than we have seen since April.

The damp dreariness of the day has washed yesterday's fall color from everything. Tree bark and leaf, rock and grass appear like photographs overexposed—colorful but not vibrant, sharp but lacking the depth that sunlight brings. Rhododendron leaves are lacquered and stiff-black under gray sky; their surfaces mirror what little light there is. Buster leaps over and I high-step through the torrent that rushes down Nameless Creek, bustling once more. Its volume of flow and of happy wet noise are welcomed after the awful drought of three years and an especially parched summer and fall. Last week's ankle high water is puppy-back high today. Creek water, usually crystal clear, has color from topsoil washed from a pasture up the ravine a mile or more away.

Goose Creek Anniversary

Last night we celebrated our third anniversary here. Three years ago, for the first time in the one hundred and twenty year history of the house, the john could be visited indoors—and in the light—in the coldest wee hours with the flick of a switch! After the six hardest months of our lives, the old shell of a house was warm and bright on that first morning here in November, 1999.

But the silence was frightening. We had lived in quiet places before, but there was an intensity to the calmness here that we had not imagined during the six months of noise and confusion to make the house livable. Now that we, in fact, lived here and the carpenters and painters and plumbers and delivery trucks were finally gone, I'll be honest: the serenity and remoteness of our new home was a little unsettling.

Just the night before we moved, still in our place on Walnut Knob, we had slept high on the edge of the Blue Ridge, up in the clouds. I wondered during the first days here if I might suffer claustrophobia, sunk beneath ridges, looking up at them rather than perched atop one looking down.

The crunch of a car passing on the road in the dark was startling; all who passed then were rank strangers, potential intruders, passing close to the house on the road just beyond our bedroom window. Those few who lived on our road were nice, hardworking folks, but rougher cut than the retirement summer home people who drove past our cabin near the Blue Ridge Parkway.

Often, cars would go by very slowly or even stop near the house with their engines running. It was only months later after meeting some of those neighbors that I learned they had stopped to admire the improvements in the old place that most thought would never see another coat of paint, much less the modern amenities it now possessed. But cars even stopped at night. Now I know why—to admire the valley that is open pasture once again. It is a wonderful sight at night, when moonlight turns the thin fog an opalescent blue and a silhouetted pair of deer browse in the tall grass. I can't fault those who passed for stopping here; I would, too.

Home is not just the house, with its new windows, wiring, freedom from outhouses, and its comfortable black porch dog. Our home is all of this, where we "live and move and have our being." Home is the high inaccessible ridges where the deer go during the daytime; it is the plot of redeemed pasture where the grasses swirl in the wind and the woodchucks chuck wood; we live in the reaches of two rocky creeks whose waters rise and fall predictably with each rain. Our new home is even the sad timber-harvested berry patch up behind the house, where the white pines are making new forest for our children's children.

It is good to be here. I wonder what I will say about our lives on this November morning three or five years down the road. Already, we are deeply rooted here, and I like to think our grandchildren and their children will love it just as we do. We will make this ours, and as I have said on many occasions, Lord willing, when we move from this house and this home, it will be in a simple pine box.

Rise and Fall

The north winds, gusty and erratic yesterday, are steady and predictable this morning. A raven takes advantage of the uniform current, faces into the wind, wings adjusted just so. He hangs motionless against the gale as if painted on the sky. Then, when he takes a notion, he turns round with the flow and tucking his wings against his body, falls like a rock, pulling exuberant out of the dive at the last moment.

I watch him repeat this rough ballet several times before I come inside, jealous of his world view. That I should learn to ride the currents of my own life with such art and joy!

Near the Source

Nameless Creek comes from darkness underground, beginning in a dozen springs a mile south. In its past, it has raged back and forth between the ridges, swollen and angry, carving our narrow valley from Appalachian stone. Today the little stream purrs along peacefully enough, cold, clear as liquid glass, on its way down mountains. It carries the smell of snow to a sandy beach on the sea. Tonight our little creek will freeze along the edges. In a month, we will hear a river embryo calling faintly from under ice and we will walk on water.

Winter Walk

The sun will be up soon, and we will be heading out for our morning walk, this week after Thanksgiving. We are now one season removed from summer and our lives have taken on a different character, a seriousness not familiar in June.

A June morning walk is a casual and spontaneous amble, and we are in no particular hurry to go or to come back. We follow our usual loop down the pasture road. We step across the creek on the dry backs of boulders in the shade of the lanky rhododendron.

We amble home north along the logging road, and use our hiking sticks to keep us from slipping in the wet grass. Now and then we stop to note a new arrival in the calendar of budding and blooming things. The air is still, heavy with the familiar smells of warm earth, fields and woods. A hundred birds sing about themselves from high in tulip poplars that are sprouting tiny leaves. At the end of our walk, the path leads downhill toward the meadow where we cross the creek once more and return home.

When winter comes, our morning walks don't end, but they are no longer a casual tiptoe through the woods. Winter walks are a deep-sea dive into cold and dark, in a submersible of wool and down. Peeking out from stocking hats like diving helmets, we trudge heavily against the stern and biting currents of polar air that wash over us like waves. Without our swaddling spacesuits, our frail pink flesh would turn blue and brittle as December leaves, and our expedition would never be heard from again.

A summer breath, outdoors or in, is little different. But with the first breathing in of winter air outdoors, you know that you have stepped out into a world that is remarkable for things missing. Winter outdoors is a play on a stage vaguely familiar, from which most of the props have been temporarily removed. Heat is only one of the absent characters. Diminished too are color, smell and the sounds and motion of living nature. Even molecules move with lethargy.

Come the play of winter, all the best lines have been spoken by autumn; and, except for the wind, there are no words.

Summer is soft, yielding and supple. Winter is hard, unyielding and brittle. You feel winter through your feet and hear it in your steps. Cold dry air has its own smell, and there is a sound that belongs to the cold of winter. It is the sound of breathing, ears muffled, holding the beat of your own heart in wool like an echo in an empty shell. No birds call; insects sleep frozen solid under bark and sod.

Winter smells of wool and of wrapped humanity inside. From beyond the thick shroud of winter clothes there is only the near-fragrance of frost. No motes of aroma escape on warm currents from spicebush, sassafras, white pine, from dank soft creek mud or pasture clover. There should be an olfactory adjective, like monochrome, to describe the lunar-stark aromasphere of winter.

Edge of Winter

Something is not right with Buster, the dog-king of Goose Creek. First one limb, then another goes lame. One day he limps and whimpers and can't stand or walk normally. Then, the next day, he seems fine.

He's not quite four years old yet—not middle aged for a Black Lab—and should be in his prime now. This morning when he came down the single step into our bedroom to wake us, as he does every day, his legs came out from under him, and he fell in a sickening thud on the bare floor. He seems so bewildered by it all and we can't tell him—or each other—that it will be alright soon. Part of his problem is pain and some is weakness in front and back legs; even his neck seems to bother him at times. The ticks were unusually bad until earlier this month, and Ann wonders about tick-borne diseases as a cause for his symptoms. I don't think this would account for the strange migrating weakness.

The pup was born within a few days of the day that we put our money down on this place. He's been part of the whole of this household on Goose Creek since it started. It doesn't seem right doing anything without him along. I miss his company when he doesn't have the energy or the will to go out with me to bring in firewood. Some days he barely lifts his head to watch me pull on my boots and jacket. This isn't like Buster.

As Ann and I notice our own slow physical decline, we live vicariously through the strength and vitality of the dog. When he races across the pasture rousting the deer from the shadows at the end of the field, our hearts run with him. We joy in his strength and agility as he pulls effortlessly up the sheer banks above the pasture road just to chase a squirrel up a tree. When he is down, we are diminished.

We got our first snow two days back—a wet one that broke branches and littered our one-lane road with limbs. Rather than drive home in the storm, Ann spent her first storm-night at the hospital where she is able to stay in an empty patient room. She has some but not all of the comforts of home there, while home grows empty and time passes oh so slowly when it's just me and the dog within these walls for days on end.

The power went out about 4:00 yesterday afternoon, during my second day here alone in the storm. I read by candle-light for a couple of hours and heated up a can of soup on the gas stove. The radio was nice until the batteries went dead. I called one of the kids on the phone just to hear another voice. By seven o'clock it was dark, my eyes and brain were tired and I was ready for bed, or at least ready for the numbness of sleep. Going to bed felt like waving the white flag of surrender. So instead, I got dressed for the cold and took the dog for a slow walk in the snow.

A half-moon was lifting through bare trees, above the eastern horizon behind thin, pink clouds. The ink-black dog cast an otherworldly shadow against the blue lunar light. In the beautiful moments here, time alone is the most wholesome and nourishing solitude.

If this new reality of mine is a journey, then I am approaching the edge of a featureless tundra just ahead—the unknown terrain of the coming winter in isolation. To get to the other side of it, I choose to be an explorer embarking on an expedition, not a lost soul wandering aimlessly in the frozen desert.

But I don't know what lies ahead. Explorers have a destination, a goal, some reason for crossing unknown lands. And a map. What are my reasons? What are the landmarks on my new map to give me bearings, and what is at its farthest edge?

January Thaw

Today we enjoy the mixed blessing of the January Thaw. It is a bit early, but why not? Every other aspect of the weather has thumbed its nose at the predictions over past months. A weatherman's air mass, we have seen, can be mutinous and surly as a spoiled teenager, and without warning, aim a high-powered wind that brings down the roof on unsuspecting Wal-mart shoppers in Texas. And in a different mood, that same bubble of air a few days farther east may decide to just sit down over Virginia as it has this week, tepid and tame as a housecat, and purr contentedly until the jet stream tickles its sensitive underbelly, and it moves lethargically on toward the Bahamas.

The January Thaw is a teaser, a complimentary packet of pretzels on the agonizingly long flight to spring. After more than a month of deep freeze and ice in December, the subsoil is still hard as iron, down to the frost line. But this week's thaw has temporarily softened the top few inches that slip and slide around under foot and tire like chocolate pudding on a rock. Pastures and fields are rutted with brown swerving parallel scars from trucks feeding livestock; cattle stand around in muddy boots, up to their elbows in pasture muck. Should the seasons relent their rebellious tirades and decide to play by the rules, the Mud Season will start for real, more or less predictably, sometime in late March.

The streets of downtown Floyd are outlined in cinders and salt, marking where the gray mounds of snow have finally vanished. The January Thaw this week has sent flake and crystal down the city drains, heading now for Little River, and from thence north through the New, and the Kanawha and Ohio, then looping back south to the Gulf of Mexico where they will retire on a beach on the Mississippi coast.

Meanwhile, a few short-sleeved human types busy themselves in the tiny heart of town on this warm January day, finding excuses to step outdoors onto solid and temporarily dry surfaces of sidewalks in the comfortable afternoon. They greet their neighbors before the real winter comes on the heels of these brief days of duplicitous temperance.

Cars and trucks along the street during the Thaw are gray-brown, the color of lost dogs, embarrassed to be seen looking so forlorn. But what's the point in taking a bath, they ask. In this short, in-between chapter that falls between pre-winter and real winter, the mud falls on the godly and the ungodly alike, so the Subaru and the farm-use truck next to it don't look all that different, mud being a great equalizer in Nature's homogenizing democracy.

Wind in winter

Last night the wind screamed overhead like a great circling bird, back and forth from ridge to ridge. Every now and then it would swoop down to clutch at our porch roof and ruffle the metal, making a strange rumbling studio-thunder sound effect. Then it would lift again and circle a thousand feet above us, coursing the high places round and round, sounding like a great locomotive caught in a switching yard right over Goose Creek.

Now summer winds throw angry tantrums like this just briefly, and only when performing the accompaniment to a summer thunder storm. A million green living leaves modulate the pitch and timbre of the wind, so that even in the summer gale there is a softness, a lifting and cleansing quality that is altogether missing from wind in winter. Summer wind appears at the height of the storm, strutting and fretting about briefly; and then it exits stage left and its pitch falls off, Doppler-like, and only a cooling breeze is left behind. I have no complaints to register against summer winds.

But winter wind arrives here irritable and there is no cheering it up. Dense and gray, heavier than air, it sinks into our valley like a glacier of broken glass, pushing down against hard and frozen earth, and it will not relent. When the wind howls at midnight, I dream of the Old Man Winter of children's books, his cheeks bloated full, lips pursed and brow furrowed, exhaling a malevolent blast below at frail pink children in wet mittens.

If you listen, you may think you hear a tone to the roar of January wind, a discrete pitch of a note that you could find on a piano keyboard. But this isn't so. In the same way all rainbow colors blend to make white light, January wind is the sound of all tones that nature can create, at once together as the Old Man overhead blows through a mouthpiece formed of ridge and ravine, across reeds of oak and poplar trunks.

Winter wind is the white noise of January that won't go away.

Rivers Below

When the kids were small, we turned page after page in the amazing picture books by David Macaulay, including one called *Underground*. I don't know what the kids thought of it, but I was mesmerized by the author's architectural cross-section of a big city. The vantage point was looking up at a downtown cityscape from its roots, showing the detail of what was underground below it. His images revealed a world of pipes and pilings, tunnels and sewers, and processes that go on under our urban feet, day and night, to keep a city working—a world necessary and real, but out of mind and sight. I never saw any city the same way after experiencing the new reality from the pictures in that book.

Years later, we moved to a small farm in Wythe County where we had a pasture fenced in for cattle but no water for them to drink. The old spring sat against the edge of a shallow bowl that long ago had filled with mud and more recently had been invaded by willows and overgrown by alders. Over the course of a month, with a mattock and shovel and long metal pole I gouged and clawed further and further back into the muddy bank, until finally one day, I struck the limestone bedrock. But there was no water there. The next day, that spot was darker than the dry soil around it. With more digging, this wet patch showed a slow visible seep. I abandoned the pick and shovel for a hand trowel and heavy screw driver as I worked back into the soft limestone. After weeks of teasing away the rock and mud, I arrived at the excavation one morning to find a miraculous flow had appeared! Soon this underground water filled a pond where our children floated on rafts on a summer day and ice skated on its mirrored surface in winter. Water out of stone—the nearest thing to magic I have known.

There is a "city" of structure under my feet here in this very spot where I write, many miles from civilization. Carry Mr. Macaulay's camera down a thousand feet below our pasture on the banks of the headwaters of Goose Creek, and above the impervious core of ancient rock you will see a vast blanket of stone full of tiny pores and cracks. Through it run creeks and rivers in the dark. Contained by it are canyons, caves and lakes filled with ancient rains.

In places this water-filled layer comes to earth, to the world above ground, and cold subterranean water oozes and flows from clefts in the side of snow-covered hills. Finding each other in low places, united by gravity, ribbons of mountain spring water merge and flow together and cut their way through the very rock from which they were born.

See this water of Goose Creek, rushing past with such hurry. It will someday rise from sea to cloud to move again over mountains. From under these ridges will pour light and sound into creeks flowing past those who will stand on these banks, careless above river worlds underground.

ICE: Figments and Formations

You hear of remote country places where so little goes on that the locals sit around and watch the grass grow. I'm here to tell you that I have experienced the winter counterpart of that mindless rapture, and of this fact I am not ashamed. For the past two months, I have watched the ice grow and morph in our creek, and it has been a most beautiful, amazing and confusing hobby. I do not know what I am seeing, cannot explain it, and lament the fact that I have missed fleeting opportunities to capture rare photographic images to remind me of all the wonders I have and have not seen.

Witnessed: crystal stalactites of ice that look every bit as if they were formed from the roof of a limestone cave. And sharp transparent shards like snowflakes that form a visible fringe along the edge of the creek. I have seen the results of something like snow that forms overnight, six inches deep, right along the water's surface in a zone of supersaturated frozen air. This magic leaves a white-spongy pad of airy creek-snow on the rocks, even on mornings when it has not snowed on land the night before.

Fluted. Filigreed. Lacey. Cancellous. Clear as crystal glass, blue-green as a glacier. Granular and rough over here at the top of this rocky ledge; and just there in the shadow of the bluff, a smooth, flat sheet protects itself by reflecting the pale pastel light of a weak winter sun. Ice buttons and balls, goblets and goblins decorate the drab grasses at creek's edge with bright colorless ornaments. Air bubbles under glass move rodent-like downstream, in a warren of liquid and crystal.

Seeds in the Snow

It is the time of year, in some parts of the country, when a body can begin to lose hope; a time when the White Witch of Narnia rules, and it is "always winter but never Christmas." This is a season of gray mud outside and gray walls inside, of too much knowledge of the same rooms since early December. Snow by now is no longer beautiful or exciting, blue skies and the sound of song-birds are not even a memory.

I felt foolish in my rubber boots as I stepped over the fence wire that the deer have broken down around the garden. I stood there in the mud yesterday in the falling sleet in the middle of our garden where once there were living things, thinking:

Let me have life about me that is green. Resurrect in me the knowledge and hope that things will grow in rows and clusters, will flower and fruit in gold and red, will spill yellow pollen into the air and smell like bread baking. Let me have hope that here, where I stand in frozen mud and slush around my ankles, I will feel the warm sun on my neck and hear bees buzzing in the corn tassels above my head. Give me rich, crumbling soil beneath my feet and let me hold a handful of sweet earth, fragments of the composted remains of last year's harvest—a better soil than when we started this little patch. Days are longer now, if not warmer. Gardening season is not a cruel myth. Plan. Anticipate. Plant seeds in your mind.

Honor of Wood

Yesterday, in the weak sun of mid-March, I split kindling, standing in a thaw of mulch that squished like a soggy sponge under my rubber boots. The day was warm enough that, after a few minutes, I was down to my flannel shirt with the sleeves rolled up. Here in the heel-end of the winter woodpile are remnants of wood dry now for more than three years—sassafras, dogwood, sourwood. I relocated all of it here from Walnut Knob, truckload at a time, when we moved from across the county in the fall of 1999. Now we're dipping into the wood archives, and I know the history of every piece. I burn it with some reluctance and much reverence.

Into the stove this morning I tossed a few pieces of an old barn log that had been notched by hand a hundred or more years ago. The log was cut, I'm sure, from these hillsides when the barn was being built. We had put several of these logs aside when we cleaned out the barn, thinking it would be a shame to burn them. But they were gradually just going to rot and would do no one any good merely decaying along the edge of the pasture. Even so I regretted turning to ash and heat this remnant of lives once lived here, the final trace of families who had built this house and harvested and used the wood from this valley long before we came to know and love it.

Wood is more than a mere commodity of country living. I understand the Indian hunter's gratitude expressed to a fallen deer, killed so his family could eat. I feel a similar appreciation for the wood I burn. I honor the strength it holds in its concentric rings and the power of sunlight stored in its silent, seasonal growth spurts in the forest. I see in every piece of it the Creator's wisdom that turns sunlight and carbon into heartwood and leaf. Wood is a miraculous product of nature that has been so wonderfully adaptable to mankind's needs, so abundant and ordinary that we might easily undervalue its true worth to us.

I stop my work and pick up a piece of kindling, inhaling deeply: of the astringent medicinal smell of walnut; cherry wood, sweet like childhood cough syrup; sassafras, smooth and spicy like hard stick candy; and oak smelling sour, of November frost with overtones of fungus and smoke. The wood I burn is a gift and a blessing—stacked, drying and fragrant—no less than our daily bread.

The time will come not so many winters from now when I will have to pay somebody else to deliver a winter's worth of firewood for us. It will not be the same then, heating with wood I didn't bring in from my own forest. Burning bought wood will be like eating vegetables from the store, imported from California. The nutritional content of store-bought and home-grown is probably about the same, but the taste of homegrown is sweeter from the labor that has gone into it. Purchased firewood will generate as many BTUs of heat as the wood I cut myself. It will heat me but it will not warm me in the same way as wood cut, split, stacked and stoked by these willing but weaker hands.

Unplugged

The older I get, the more I think of my senses as one of life's most marvelous gifts. The more that vision and hearing gradually decline, the dearer they become, and the more I want to indulge them in the minutiae of the close-at-hand. To hold on to what hearing I haven't already lost, I wear earplugs every time I use the chain saw. They block the worst of the engine noise, but even with them in place, it is not nothing that I hear.

The two-cycle sputter of the engine is muted to my ears but its percussion passes through my hands, through my bones. With the plugs in place, the throb of my own pulse and the sound of breathing echo as if in a small, closed room. Wind howls across the plastic line that keeps the two earplugs together in a wonderfully exaggerated made-for-Hollywood sound effect as I cut up the firewood for the stove.

I have used this same pair of earplugs for so long that the airplane orange is now a faded pink. I yank them out as soon I shut off the saw. And unplugged, the ordinary, easily unheard Goose Creek audiosphere is born out of the muffled silence.

There: the mewling caw of two crows flying counter-clockwise swooping circles above me as I look up. They follow the unhurried path of a magnificent red tail hawk backlit by morning sun. If this raucous remonstration makes the crows feel better, it obviously has no appreciable deterrent effect on the hawk who barely changes the camber of his wings to accommodate their clumsy attack. His thin "tee-deeeer" trails off into the distance as he disappears over the neighbor's ridge with his two cawing escorts.

Closer, just at the top of my cap, a tiny tornado-swirl of midges hums while they weave their loopy spiral rise-and-fall dance along an invisible axis not far from my right ear. Do they hear each other's Doppler comings and goings in their vertical column of space?

And there is the sound of water when the earplugs come out. I don't even hear it most of the time. So common-place, it rarely registers as anything to bother being aware of, like the feel of the shirt on my back: it's just there.

But when the plugs come out, against the soft shushing of my breathing and pulse, the rambunctious rush of the creek seems larger than life—crisp, close, and coming from all around. I hear undertones of its rippling babble ricocheting off the house; I can distinguish the trickle of the branch from the louder rush of Goose Creek from the wind in the bare branches.

I hate having those pink plugs in my ears. But it's almost worth it, just to be able to take them out and hear again. And to listen to the ordinary.

Field of Dreams

Four years ago March, the only level acres we own were choked with 13-year-old white pine trees. We suppose the planters were paid by the tree, the owners of this land intending to harvest them as Christmas trees. They put in far too many trees for the space, and planted them too close together. After the planting, the pines were neglected, and grew tall and spindly in long dreary rows. Each tree's branches were bare almost to the top, starved of light by the nearest neighbors. Rank and file they grew on the flood plain of Nameless Creek, and on around the bend of the valley.

Three years ago, March, the neighbors with the backhoe began the slow process of pushing down the pines that were by then twenty feet tall. They would soon be too dense and heavy to deal with if we didn't go ahead and remove them. Through the spring and into the summer, as we put back little bits of "extra" money, the boys would come and doze, then burn another acre or fraction of an acre—whatever we could afford. By the fall, what had been a ragged pine thicket was a bare, rough and muddy plane. We imagined it green and inviting someday. In October, we bought 300 pounds of rye. Ann and I scattered it by hand on a gray day, with a strong wind at our backs—six acres of seeds—and waited for the rains to come.

The next March, two years ago, the rye came up ever so slowly from the cold ground. Then, with the warm days of May and June, it surged up waist high and our muddy flat began to look like a pasture. In July, at dusk when ground fog hung over the valley floor, deer moved like ghosts in the shoulder high grain.

One year ago this month, our neighbor came and put down lime. In May, he broadcast a pasture mix of orchard grass and clover. In the fall, seventeen large round bales lay scattered along our new pasture, a kind of organic Stonehenge.

Ann, the dog and I walk up the field, along the creek and back every day. The green peace there feels as if it has always been just so, waiting for us to come into the open, our field of dreams.

From the far end of the grassy floodplain, we look back down the narrow valley over the flat earth and see the barn and north ridge, and at night from the middle of the clearing, golden light glows from inside our house. And overhead, more of Heaven swirls around me than I can comprehend.

Breath of Spring

The pasture grass is knee high, taller than the tops of my black rubber barn boots. The blue violets are almost hidden by the ranker ground coverings. Mayapple is tall enough to shade a rabbit and shows its waxy blossoms if you get down on your knees to see them; and the pasture loop is about to get its first mowing of the season.

Our foot path that Ann push-mows begins at the barn, goes up the valley along the pasture road, and loops back around the outside perimeter of the field. Then there are lesser branches of the mowed path on the house side of the creek—a two-foot-wide swath that totals at least three-quarters of a mile.

This morning, walking in the knee-high dew-wet grass where the tended path will soon reappear, we heard the first wood thrush song echoing between the ridges; and now as dusk falls, there are two of them. Ann called me to the back door just now. Listen: in the distance, up back where the blackberries grow—the first whippoorwill. The haunting, melancholy sound reverberates in the natural bowl to the north where the branch begins.

At last the days have been warm enough so that I am startled now and then by the smell of spring—not any particular and definable smell but rather a kind of teabag steeping of winter's gray dregs, the aroma of green things —mosses, new petals and liverworts—and warm dark earth.

The Green Holes

Where our land ends, the Wild Places begin. Picture an angular "V" five hundred feet on a side. At the bottom of the V-shaped gorge runs a tumbling creek that has no name, gurgling, flowing past, dropping over, curling around jumbled fern-covered boulders. Strewn over it all are broken trees—massive hemlocks and pines fallen, broken away from thin soil by Hurricane Hugo in 1989, and a couple of bad ice storms after that. Fifty feet above this falling branch runs an old postal road (still called the "New Road" by the local folk) on which a man on horseback once delivered saddlebags of mail from the thriving farming community of Simpsons to the remote families that inhabited our once-prosperous valley. No one goes on this rough road anymore, except a couple of slow-moving middle-aged walkers, and a dog.

We walk that handmade road from time to time, admiring Nameless Creek below as it falls from ledge to pool, falls upon falls. It's far too steep to scramble down those banks and we find ourselves saying "one day we need to start from our place, where the banks aren't so steep, and just walk the creek up into the gorge here." And yesterday, I did just that.

The old timers drive up the county road through our valley and notice that the home place has been given a new life. They know this land better than we do, having lived around here all their long lives, and they stop to chat. "I'll bet you enjoy dipping in the old green holes up the creek there. We use ta gather and swim in 'em back when we was kids. Some was deep enough to dive inta," they tell me wistfully.

"Well, no sir" I say, "The deep plunge pools have pretty well filled in with silt and creek gravel since you knew them. There wasn't much farming upstream, I reckon, when you came here as a little boy. The water is only deep as our knees in just a few places now, but it's pretty, just the same."

Still, it is easy for me to imagine slipping into one of those dark green-crystal pools under arching rhododendron and Laurel, shedding all encumbrances and cares; gasping with the first shock of cold; feeling on my skin the sting of water the temperature of the very earth, slipping down, down and under emerald water in a wild place under a warm blue summer sky.

Summer Symphony

This has been a wonderful day of sun, a reprieve from weeks of spring drizzle, welcomed on the eve of the summer solstice. A cold front passed through and carried away the blue haze, so edges are vibrant-razor-sharp. The green-ness soothes the eye today under an achingly blue sky. I had almost forgotten.

While the colors *were* remarkable, it was the sound of this day that made me take notice. Standing at the edge of the creek in the warm sun in the amphitheater of our valley, sound reverberated in layers, bottom to top—the creek rumbling below, a thousand incessant insects stridulating in the middle, while the northwest wind above played the ridges in the treble clef.

The creeks are risen and clear; much of the water enters the flow from underground. Recent rains have forced cold clear water from deep below the surface into the swollen stream—enough water to call it a torrent, and it is raucous, in a hurry. If you could stand at the shore of the ocean and record the sound of breakers, then take out pauses between waves—this is the sound that roars along the valley floor today. Breakers without a break, the bass undertones in this valley full of sound.

The seventeen-year cicadas relentlessly wax and wane their nasal love songs, although now and then the singing males all stop together at once, just for a moment. They preen circumspectly before getting back to their seductive songs. I'm certain they expect at any moment a lured lady locust will climb up to their singing perch and make arthropodic whoopie. It must be a most orgasmic event—to have waited seventeen years for this very moment. I wonder: if you listened closely, could you hear the instant of those little whoops when the next generation of earth-sleeping insects is conceived, followed by a satisfied sigh, just days before death?

On top of the ridges the wind becomes visible as a million leaves race just ahead of its force, like the standing wave that crowds perform in perfectly timed sequence at football games. Before me, a stadium filled with soft leaves. They rise in unison along the leading edge of the wind; they sit back down as it passes, only to stand and cheer again and again.

The cool air today is light, full of energy and ozone. It has come here all the way from the tundra, never breathed before, save by a few caribou, and fewer wolves. The sound of wind in summer treetops brings a multitude of boreal voices, a soft rushing whisper that lacks the shrill whine inflicted in December by this wind's winter relatives traveling over Nameless Creek though bare branches.

Lucid Daydreams

I become very still sitting on the front porch on a calm and tepid summer day. I am asking my mind to wander free from limits, from reason and the burden of gravity. It is time to cast off.

Eyes lose focus, the body rises weightless, and I possess power over time. Nature is at my whim and I call on the century-old maple tree to repeat before my eyes in five minutes and in reverse history a hundred years of growth. I bid it stop at the moment it entered the ground as a winged seed. Then I command it to grow from seed to shade tree again. This I repeat over and over until I become saturated with the details of how a tree twists and lurches and spreads as it grows old, and the converse as it grows young again. And later I may cast this spell on different kinds of trees up the valley noting differences in the choreography.

Farther down the valley where I wonder without leaving my chair, fireflies emit pulses of light and also give out tiny corresponding throbs of percussive sound, a barely perceptible drum beat. Their language reverberates between deep purple hillsides at midnight. Is there a rhythm here—a pattern of light and sound, a message that my senses cannot quite make out?

I am still, still moving; still but wandering this new-alien terrain. The soil in our pasture and woods becomes transparent, but it gives shelter and substrate for a legion of insects and burrowing creatures visible, suspended underfoot. Each kind of being has its own unique bioluminescence and I walk spellbound on the surface of invisible ground, above endless thousands of subterranean animals I have never known that swim or float, as if under depth of water.

I walk Nameless Creek at the very edge of this world. I bend and lift one rock, then another—of rounded gray granite or pink quartz; of angular shale or sheets of slate—and each stone I see in its context of time, can go back to its life at its origin to the Very Beginning. I can follow the journey back to its source ten thousand miles and eons from here, and watch as sharp Paleozoic mountains melt into round-shoulder Blue Ridges of home.

Part Two:

Leaf, Feather and Fur

Tiny Links in a Delicate Chain

> To make a prairie it takes a clover and one bee—
> One clover, and a bee,
> And revery.
> The revery alone will do
> If bees are few. ~ Emily Dickinson

I don't imagine the average person has noticed or would much care. Farmers and orchardists know it, and it is front page news for home gardeners. One of our chief agents in pollination for a vast variety of fruit, nut, and vegetable crops—the honey bee—is essentially lost from the wild. Emily, bees are few.

In the garden this morning the noisy drone of squash bees caught my attention. The fat-bodied specialists were busy working the big gold blossoms along the ground under oversized leaves. Many of them carried enough pollen on their back legs that I could see their amber saddlebags from ten feet away. Seeing pollen sacks on squash bee legs made me think how long it had been since I had watched a *honeybee* pollinate an apple blossom, or blackberry, or sunflower.

Almost all native honeybee hives are gone since the 1980s because of infestations of varroa mites (an ectoparasite) and tracheal mites (which live inside the insect's breathing passages). Antibiotic-protected hives are hauled around to orchards and farms where these disease-protected bees perform the task once done by bees from wild hives. Honeybees are a childhood memory. Growing up in the Deep South, we went barefoot for six months every year, and the sweet clover in the grass was the source of at least a few bee stings every summer.

In the midst of my pondering, I glanced up overhead at the corn tassels to see how tall the stalks were now (over 8 feet!) and to my surprise, there were at least a dozen honeybees! They were gleaning pollen from the anthers that hang like tiny rust-red sausages from the male parts up top. Corn is wind pollinated and doesn't need the bees, but the bees need the pollen as food for their young. We're a far piece from the nearest beekeeper, so there must be at least one surviving natural hive nearby. I wonder if I could follow these drones home as they leave the corn? Early in the morning, when the garden is backlit by the sun just coming over the ridge, I should be able to see which direction they head—making a "bee-line" for home and honey.

And so today I know that honeybees live with us on Goose Creek, and my world is more complete. The buzz of this small and once abundant link in the chain of the natural order of things reminds me of our prairie: a complete and interdependent whole of soil and rain, heat and light, insect and flower. And reverie.

The Season of Spiders

It is now officially the middle of summer—not the weatherman official but the Goose Creek local-native official middle of the summer. And so it will be six more weeks until fall begins. This practical fact few people know, because they don't know how to read the spiders.

Every morning we walk the AT—the Annie Trail that she keeps mowed around the edge of the pasture. We walk along the edge of the field, then cross the creek to follow the old logging path we call the "middle road" through the rhododendrons and mountain laurels and mixed hardwoods. Yesterday the small spiders of mid-summer were actively "bridging": extruding their invisible one-strand silks on the air currents across gaps between tree branches, blackberry canes, and especially across open spaces, like footpaths. This spider event is one of the hopeful signs of fall to come, and I am glad to see them, if annoyed by their attempts to snare me as food.

It is just at this time of year that a spider stick is essential on the trails. Without it, you'd better be prepared about every twenty feet to stop, mutter to yourself, and swipe your hand ineffectually across your brow to remove the invisible stand of microscopic spider filament from your forehead and eyelashes. Occasionally you'll find yourself staring cross-eyed at a small nondescript arachnid dangling from the bill of your cap—no real threat here, just the less-than-wonderful sensation that living legged ornaments are hanging from you like tinsel from a Christmas tree.

The person who walks first carries the stick (or more commonly, a broken bough of a spicebush) out front like a scepter, to intercept the spider silk before it becomes festooned across the nose and cheeks. Ann and I take turns with this duty. But it is almost always the dog who goes first on these walks. We invent clever imaginary ways to attach something to Buster (a rooftop TV antenna, for instance) to outfit him to clear away the webs before we get to where he has already been.

In four weeks, the spiny spiders (genus *Micrathena*) will show up. These are very visible, ornate, chunky spiders that live in a rolled leaf at the highest point of their web. They spin more elaborate webs across the path, and without the stick, these bizarre but harmless little monsters often end up perched on the rim of your glasses. You really need that spider stick. In a few weeks, the inch-thick, round-bodied orb-weavers too will be stringing their snares across the path, set out to capture a hiker. It is rumored that just one average sized pedestrian can feed an orb-weaver family for an entire year!

Summer will have ended in my almanac when the balloon spiders appear floating tethered to bright threads in the September sky. Airborne spiders are a true marvel that too few have witnessed, and I look forward to seeing them and telling myself their story again in the early fall.

In Praise of August

It is August at last. True, there may not yet be much difference in day or nighttime temperatures. But here in the mountains, we can typically expect a tantalizing preview of the coming season during the first half of this month. There are signs of fall already, if you know what to look for.

Many of autumn's wildflowers have emerged, though they are small and inconspicuous and most haven't blossomed yet. It will be another few weeks before you'll notice them as you drive along the back roads. But it is part of the pattern of things that the goldenrod, Joe Pye weed, and ironweed will become the dominant vegetation soon, adding rich deep yellow, dusky mauve and royal purple to the palette of color in every meadow and pasture border.

Soon, the starlings will grow restless. They'll congregate nervously in a few trees here and there, as if they are both attracted and repulsed by each other in a mob of squawking voices. Not one among them knows where they are headed or why—only that something big is about to happen. The instinct to migrate must be a powerful itch.

It won't be long before an occasional Monarch butterfly shows up on Goose Creek, passing by in loops and glides. In ones and twos, they will lift on the rising heat, winged wisps of will, bound at first in no particular direction and free of hurry. Then, later in the month and unfailingly west, they will glide resolutely toward winter roosts in central Mexico—a pilgrimage in such numbers that their combined weight will break the branches out of their roosting trees.

We should be looking for woolybear caterpillars to turn up in the next week or two, crossing the roads of Floyd County in large numbers in their brown and black three piece suits. I've given up trying to divine the harshness of winter from the ratio of the wooly worm's colors. The message I carry away from their thick furry wool is simply that it will be more or less cold by and by. A thick black or brown coat like theirs will come in mighty handy then, though it's hard to imagine that in August's heat.

This month, the locusts and walnuts, last to put on their spring leaves, will be first to take them off. Harbingers of fall, the feather-pinnate leaves of sumac will be among the first to go orange along the wooded roadsides, followed soon by Virginia creeper's five-fingered leaves climbing red up the trunks of trees along the edges of our woods. Both these chameleon color changes will happen well ahead of what will show up higher overhead, later in the poplars, hickories and maples.

Some of the fallness that I will feel this week or next has nothing to do with changes in the visible signs of fall. It will come perhaps from an imperceptible sense of the loss of mere moments each day. In the same way that our inner alarms awaken us promptly every morning, my seasonal alarm sounds the call of fall this week. I'm confident that if you blindfolded me, spun me around ten times, and placed me anywhere on the calendar, I could tell you "this is early August" by the feel of it alone. But then, there are also the smells of the coming season in the air.

On such a day as this in early autumn, I breathe in the new aromas that August alone can give—the scent of sweet clover and hay, of corn stalks going but not quite gone by—a potpourri of plant matter in profusion, baked dry by the summer sun. The aromas of monarda and pennyroyal, spicebush and sassafras were overpowered by the sweet smell of pasture pollen in mid July, but not so today. I will be sniffing for their faint traces and will stop often in the garden for deep drafts of fall-flavored air.

This week, or the next, I will look up and declare "that is a fall sky!" when the round piled and billowed clouds of summer for a day or two give way to clouds streaked and smeared, thin, high and stretched with the ends turned up, against a turquoise sky.

Fall will make a few short sorties in August, then retreat, and return again to stay longer each visit. "To everything there is a season, and a time to every purpose under Heaven." It is time for fall, even though the season has not yet quite arrived.

Every Drought Ends with a Good Rain

The cool breeze is welcomed today, a respite from the unrelenting heat of summer. But the wind and sun are also the enemy because they carry away what little moisture remains in the pasture grasses, forest and creeks. More than that, even the underground waters that are the source of streams like Nameless Creek are silently ceasing to flow. More water has evaporated from tree and soil to the thin clouds overhead than has fallen from sky to earth during the past three months.

No current moves the surface of the creek, though minnows still stir the shrinking pools in a claustrophobic frenzy. They struggle to find edible specks in what little water remains in the shallow depressions here and there along the drying creek bed. We are in the midst of a sad and awful drought. There is a tendency to take the malice of this dry, parched weather personally, but we should keep the cycles of nature in perspective.

Our valley is a tiny crease carved by water in the more recent stages of Appalachian mountain erosion. The core of the Blue Ridge formed nearly a billion years ago when land masses collided, lifting up a massive bulge of fire-hardened rock. It is difficult to conceive now that these green and gentle mountains began as a rocky dome, higher and more craggy and hostile than today's Rockies. Millennia passed like seconds on nature's clock, and water in unbelievable floods has worn away the old rock, one granite grain at a time. Time and water have done their work and smoothed away the roughness of these old mountains. Fragments of those ragged summits of stone now lie in pasture rock, beach sand and delta soil. All that remains of that former high magnificence are these soft and rounded, green, moist and water-worn remnants we call our Appalachian mountains.

One has only to dig down a few inches over by the barn to know that river cobbles by the tens of thousands have been left there. And there they lie buried in the sandy soil, washed down Nameless Creek as it flows together with Goose Creek not a hundred feet from where I sit. These two creeks tumbling down from those ancient mountaintops have cut against the resistant rock of the east ridge of our valley, then the west, then back again—each time widening the valley floor by imperceptible inches in hundreds of years—an unthinkably long time to our mortal perspective, a flash of time in a million years of eternal wind and sun, frost and floods.

Floods are cataclysmic, sudden, drastic and evident in their consequences. Drought like this is chronic and insidious. It drains life invisibly, quietly, leaving no record in the sands of geology's time. But it is an abundance of water that has carved the hollow of the creek bed and made the valley wide—not water's absence. It is an abundance of water that has nurtured the broad-leaved forest that covers these mountain hillsides and allowed them to persist in this leafy biome. Drought has not formed this landscape, and it seems reasonable to have hope that it will not subdue it now.

We will miss the rains for a few more weeks, for maybe one more season, or two. But we must learn to see the cycles of wet and dry as the land sees it, and be patient. If history is any lesson, water will tell the story.

Jewels In the Rough

The seasons of spring, summer and early fall at our house are marked as much by the flowers that come and go as they are by mere numbers on the calendar. Like old friends, they always visit at the same time every year and take their places in the same seats at the table—our wet stream borders, pasture margins, deep woods. Over the years, wildflowers have become good friends; I love to see them come, and hate to see them go.

The spotted jewel weed that popped up three weeks ago here and there blooms in every moist depression now, and, like the rest of us, seems happy for what little rain we have finally seen here in the last week. Although the brilliant orange flower of this plant could account for its common name, it is, in fact, the way that water beads up on the leaves like silver jewels that gives it this descriptive name. Where it grows, it typically does so in abundance. Finding a dense stand of jeweled leaves on a moist early morning creates the illusion of a gossamer gown hung secretly at the edge of the forest, adorned with thousands of round mirrored sequins.

The flower's shape is what botanists call "strongly zygomorphic." This means that there is only one plane that can pass through the flower to create mirror images, rather than the four, five, or more lines of symmetry seen in many flowers. This fact, together with the bright orange-red color, would make me suspect (if I didn't already know) that this flower is hummingbird pollinated, though moths and butterflies, with their long curled sipping mouthparts, can also get at the nectar housed deep in the spurred part of the flower. The individual flowers hang on the merest thread, and in the least wind, the whole plant oscillates with orange and silver spangles.

Jewel weed, *Impatiens capensis*, is handy to have around, for both practical and aesthetic purposes. Early in its growth, the stem is succulent, meaning it is mostly water, and consequently, translucent as if made of pale, milk-green glass. We pick a few of these early stems and put them in the freezer. Later in the summer when we most certainly will come in contact with poison ivy, yellow jackets, and stinging nettle, we'll put those frozen stems to good use on stings and itches. Jewel weed grows in just the same places as nettle, and when rubbed on these skin irritations, it takes out the fire. Unfortunately, it does not do much good on the terrible sting I got last week from the saddleback caterpillars my bare arms found on the corn leaves; their stinging hairs become embedded in the skin like microscopic poison splinters.

Another common name for the plant is worth noting. These plants are also called touch-me-not. Don't let the name put you off. It is not so called because it is in any way noxious or dangerous, but because of the behavior of its seedpods. The elongated ear-of-corn shaped seed capsules grow up to an inch long. Each consists of four long flaps that press close together to make up the pod. As the pods dries and the seeds inside begin to mature, pressure builds up in the flaps, more so on the outside than the inside of each flap. Consequently, when the pods are touched by an animal (or a small child encouraged to do so by a tricky adult who knows to expect the sudden, tiny pop), the pod opens explosively, ejecting seeds a few feet away from the parent plant, spreading itself into new soil.

The ejected seeds when mature and brown have a nutty taste and crunch. Our children enjoyed being startled all over again by the exploding seeds as they would catch some to nibble on each August. Once they had the idea that maybe these little mock-nuts would be good in cookies in place of pecans. So, we baked a batch and substituted jewel weed seeds. Eaten right out of the oven, the cookies were soft, moist, and delicious. We took the lot of them to our neighbor across the gravel road. The next time we saw her at church, she said "Those cookies were mighty good, but what were those little pebbles you put in them?"

Discovery: when the touch-me-nuts dry out again as the cookies cool, they turn hard as rocks. We were glad nobody broke a tooth.

When this odd flower dangles its hanging flowers along our creek and branch, we know that it will only be another month until we will fire up the woodstove. On a crisp, early October morning, August wildflowers will have strutted their hour on the stage, and be gone. Along with the other autumn regulars, they are the ticks on our seasonal clock, markers of the procession of seasons along Goose Creek—budding, flowering, blooming and dying, all in good time.

Blueberry Hills

We have just discovered that wild huckleberries are growing on the spine of our steepest ridge. And they are almost ripe now in late August. This means that fall cannot be far away. But when I think of high places and blue berries of autumn, it is another hillside and time that I recall most clearly.

When we lived further west in Virginia and the children were small, we never missed our late August trip to Grayson Highlands State Park to pick blueberries. Now we are two hours drive from the berries, but even so, they would be worth the travel. The sweetness of Highlands berries is remembered not just because of their sweet-tart flavor.

Today we could pick our own tiny berries from just across the road. But I'd love to return to Grayson Highlands because it is a special place in all the world to us. Its windswept rocky vistas have a haunted feel to me; there is a Presence there. I do not know why. But I do know that the hair on my arms stood up when we saw the Highlands of Scotland last year. I thought "This is where I have belonged, and Grayson Highlands points me HERE. I know this place and it is home."

I don't believe in reincarnation but have the sense that I have lived, or should have lived, in just such a place. This seems odd coming from a fella raised in Alabama. So, that is the canvas on which this tale of berries and maps is painted. The blueberries represent a private belonging to those high places where they grow best.

If I cannot go bodily, a journey of imagination aided by a good map is my second choice of travel to favorite terrain. The blueberry-picking highlands in Grayson County was one of the first places I visited when I got my new 3-D topographic map software not long ago. Seeing the wavy lines close-pressed on pale greens and browns brought back memories other than the berries. There was the night I spent alone on Pine Mountain beyond Massie Gap, watching the autumn fog creep up the heathered flanks quietly, like a cat in slippers; it curled around me in my tent well into the next morning. I remember the time I was trapped in a summer storm there at 5000 feet, again in my tent, holding up the poles against 50 mph winds, realizing that there were *no seconds* between lightning flash and gut-thudding thunder. Another time, I became hopelessly lost, alone on the Appalachian Trail as it passes through the park, alone in the frozen fog of a January day. I finally stumbled upon the rail fence and followed it thankfully back to the warmth and sanctuary of my truck—the only one parked at Grayson Highlands that raw day. Most people had better sense.

The bushes in the high elevation of the Park are so tall that you will see folks picking from horse-back! Some of the berries are as big as your thumbnail, and you can pick hands-full at a time. We counted on a gallon or more an hour per person. With the tops (but not the handles) out of milk jugs, these berry buckets looped through our belts, and we could pick two-fisted. When the milk carton got too heavy that we'd start to lose our drawers, we transferred the berries to a five gallon bucket.

The very best berry bushes are found—well, we have our secret places, discovered after years of wandering the hillsides in late August to early September. I remember exactly where to go, now that I have seen the maps again. I read the contour lines like a man reads an old letter from a good friend, his voice remembered in the handwriting. The map's lines evoke the dank musty-sour smell of the Appalachians in the die-back and fragrant decay of early fall. They bring back the ripe blue aroma of berries warming in the bucket.

Sweeter than berries are the gathered memories of friends and family that have shared this fall ritual with us. We were right there on the map, high up on the saddle of Massie Gap where, after a day of berry picking, we sat on thrones of ancient granite, sharing a bottle of wine, the wind to our backs and views before us as far as a week from Wednesday, all the way into Carolina. From that high place, we were blessed with the sense of full possession of our bearings in time and place, wearing blueberry stains all around our happy mouths.

By Any Other Name

The weeds have brought me to my knees, and I am about to concede defeat. The intentional plantings inside the fence are poking along, but the weeds get taller as I watch. I am tempted to adopt a philosophy you might call jujitsu gardening: you let the momentum of your opponent work to your advantage. It occurred to me that I should consider canning the lamb's quarters and purslane that volunteers inside the fence, since those two edible weeds are doing so exceptionally well with no effort at all on my part.

My gardening obsession this summer has been to pull the weeds before they spawn another generation of the same. But now with the rain, they threaten to get ahead of my efforts, and there is one plant especially I don't seem to be able to subdue. I learned its local name from an elderly farmer back in Wytheville long ago, but it took me months to figure out how it is known to science.

"Now that'n there is gallant soldiers," he told me, between spits of Red Man, as we surveyed my hopeful garden. "Hit'll take off and spread seeds all over, so ya wanna get that'n out quick-like."

Gallant soldiers? Hmmm. Generally you can see a trait in the plant that leads to the common name (which may vary from one county and even from one holler to the next). Consider black-eyed susan that has the black center, like an eye; touch-me-not has the exploding seed pod; poison ivy—lord'll make you itch; and there is the soft-leaved plant that I used to tell our kids was called "mountain toilet paper" (mullein) though that was my own personal common name for it. But gallant soldiers to describe the tiny, white, five-petaled flowers on spindly stalks? I took it to be a local name. Some of these regionally contrived descriptors are creative and colorful, if taxonomically confusing. I've heard other new ones since moving to Floyd County.

Back when I managed the clinic in the old Harris Baker furniture store on Main Street, I had a patient who had been injured when a tree limb fell on him. He worked for the Park Service. As I applied ultrasound to his injured shoulder, he was lamenting how much time the roadside crew had to spend clearing "those rangy trees" from the

Blue Ridge Parkway right-of-way. I asked him what tree he was talking about.

"We call 'em lancers" he said. I prodded him for details about the leaf, bark, and growth habit of "lancers" because frankly, in all my botanizing, I'd never heard of it. He finally got around to saying that lancers had a soft, corky center and that it smelled something awful. I asked if by any chance it smelled anything like peanut butter and he said yes. AHA! He was talking about tree of heaven, (a.k.a. lancers), an obnoxiously-spreading, invasive non-native plant whose scientific name is the sound-alike *Ailanthus*. And thus a local common name is born.

Another patient who worked for the highway department told me he was taking the afternoon off so that he and his brother could go out in the woods near home and cut down some Baloney Wood to sell and make some money.

"Yeah, they ship it over to Japan and pay really good for it." Again, I thought I knew my trees; but this was a new one for me. I ran through the same series of questions about shape and size and habitat and so on. Finally, when he said that it had "lots of purple flowers out on the ends," the light in my head blinked on. What he had told me about there being a market for it overseas was true, but most foresters know it as *Paulownia*. Okay. Baloney is pretty close. He knew which trees to cut, and the lumber mill man that would buy it from him probably also called it baloney wood, too. As long as they understand one another, I thought.

So, my garden weed, called gallant soldiers by my neighbor, turns out to be known among botanical types as *Galinsoga*. It's an understandable adulteration of the scientific name. And I like gallant soldiers better. It's a local twist on the high-brow Latin—like science walking around in bibbed overalls. And gallant soldiers is what I will call this charging infantry of invading weeds for the rest of my gardening life, knowing I will never defeat them.

Trash Run: A Puppy Dog Tale

After a long weekend of house guests, the effluvium of hosting and toasting had reached critical mass in the back of my truck. The time had come to make a Trash Run.

The Trash Run for me is a grievous and unavoidable necessity of country living: nobody's going to come get it, and we haven't sunk so low as to just pitch it down the side of the hill off the front porch (gravity-assisted trash disposal— very popular in some areas). So once or twice a week, we give the garbage a ride to the green box dumpsters located up on the nearest hardtop road. For Buster, our black lab, this is his raison d'etre. Other than his occasional ride to Puppy Camp (our euphemism for the kennel) when we have to be away from home for a few days, the "run" is his supreme vehicular experience. This adventure must be the thing that haunts his puppy dreams when he lies asleep, whimpering with feet twitching rhythmically. I'm certain he is dreaming of the Trash Run.

A mile and seven tenths of a steep pig path of a gravel road separates our house from the dumpsters. It is a "state maintained single lane road without turnouts" — which being interpreted is to say that, if you meet somebody coming the opposite way, hope it is not on any of the nine blind curves twixt the house and the hardtop; and know that somebody is going to do a lot of fancy driving in reverse. And I always hope it is the other guy. So, Buster and I are heading slowly around the curves and climbing up out of the creek valley ever closer to the Glorious Dumpsters.

Oh he is so proud, sitting there akimbo with one haunch on the pull-down arm rest between me and him, his great black chest thrust proudly forward like the captain of a great ship, standing at the prow — a striking figure of a dog. But for Buster, the best part of vehicle travel is the Life of the Nose whereby he takes in all those exotic country smells that come into the cab of the truck through the blowing Slotted Sniffers on the dash. It must be a mind-expanding experience for a dog. It is not quite as orgasmic an experience for the driver, as the dog huffs his wet nose repeatedly into the blowing vent, which then ejects this canine wetness back onto said driver's bare legs and arms. It is, however, somewhat cooling and refreshing.

And so, we were almost to the top (I didn't mention that this road also climbs about 400 feet in 1.7 miles), making our last blind turn. And all at once filling our view was a large, boxy and colorful refrigerated truck. As fate would have it, the large square truck was full of popsicles and driven by a suddenly terror-stricken middle-aged woman. She had obviously taken a very, very wrong turn. But since we both had to slow to a crawl anyway to nudge past each other on the narrow road without exchanging paint, and since our windows were down anyway, I thought I'd be neighborly.

I said "I'll have a Dreamsicle, and my dog here, he'll have a Nutty Bar."

The lady-driver nervously feigned a half-smile and muttered something I didn't understand. As she and her truck edged slowly past me, she was rolling up her windows and locking her doors, heading inextricably deeper into what must have seemed a god-forsaken holler. Oh, she rues the day she took this shortcut, I can assure you!

We did our dirty work, Buster and I, and unloaded the entire back of the Dakota full of empty milk cartons and cans of old dried paint from upstairs, and various discards that won't be going back to college with our son anymore—now that he has finally, at long last, graduated. And then we made our way slowly back down the beautiful long and winding road through the white pine and rhododendrons, to the house.

Then, as is our custom, I got out of the truck, but Buster, he stayed behind. This is the routine—exasperating, but expected. After one of our short drives has eneded, he has remained in the truck alone for as long as an hour, with the truck doors wide open, sitting there at the helm, Buster, Dog of Destiny, a proud captain in his small but odiferous world.

A Time to Fall

It fascinates me that a leaf knows when its time has come to fall. Perhaps some combination of day length and temperature gives the signal. But maybe it's just the good taste to abort, an inner sensitivity to the needs of the whole that gives its parent tree a chance to hibernate with its blood gone underground for the winter, safe from freezing. Whatever the signal for the moment of leaf launch, I'm glad they don't all get the same idea on the same day.

First, the walnut and basswood and spicebush leaves fly in the first winds of tropical storms or sudden thunderstorms in late summer. The poplars and hickories, cherries and sumacs have the good manners to wait a while, until after a leaf has had the proper opportunity to strut its chameleon color changes during October before finally falling, drab and shriveled, in a north wind on a bleak November day.

An oak leaf will refuse to let go until December, clacking and waggling brown and brittle in the cold breeze. The serrated leaves of a smooth-boled American Beech turn almost white and become so thin and light they hang like feathers and seem to move on their own, even on a still January day. This year's beech leaf may stay on the twig until next spring's tiny new leaf evicts it, finally pushing it out and away, off into space, down to the black soil among the first of the spring mustards and violets.

Leaves enter my fantasies this time of year. I have wondered about them, individually, and as a race. If all of the leaves from the countless trees on our acres here fell and did not decompose by the following spring; if this happened year after year, how many years would it take to choke off all growth along the forest floor? Should our woods remain alive after even one year of such a calamity, which is doubtful, how many years of leaf-fall would it take to completely fill the bowl of our valley to the rim?

If all these same leaves from our small valley could by some fairy-industry be stitched together, edge to edge, would it make one huge leaf, big enough to dress all of the New River Valley or Virginia?

And if a curious person was to lie on his back in these woods for a day, could he learn to tell all the leaves to species merely by the pattern of their falling from the tree when the air is still? My hypothesis is yes, and I gladly volunteer to undertake the research.

Turtle Encounters

In the heavy drizzle of our walk this morning, the wetness was a shocking strangeness after a summer of dusty drought. Not a quick downpour, this was Gulf water flung wide by the spiraling arms of a wet, low-pressure bubble called Isidore. Strange that we name blobs of air; but it is the impact of this nothingness that makes it worthy of personification. We had no plans one way or the other that wind or wetness could mar. For us, the tropical storm seemed benign enough, a southern visitor welcomed because he came gently and left gifts of rain.

The goldenrod and jersey tea hung wet-heavy, toppling over into the footpath along the logging road. The rain itself was meager—a heavy mist that made no noise in falling. Only after it accumulated on the drip tips of hanging leaves and bare twigs did drops fall kersplat, with louder patterings as the wind gently swelled up the valley. Slender limbs lifted and fell in slow motion. Walls of wind blew fine sheets of misty rain, south to north. We were getting wet, but our walk was the usual rain-or-shine morning ritual—until we realized that we were not alone.

The dog, always the first in line on our woods-walks, stopped briefly to sniff at something down in the grass. I would have walked right past it. Brown and yellow, hidden perfectly among like-colored fallen leaves of maple, poplar, locust and spicebush, an immaculate female box turtle was minding her own business in her own world when her day took an otherworldly twist.

Terrapene carolina—the Eastern box turtle—is by far the most common turtle hereabout. Even so, we don't often see them except when they are made visible while crossing roads—or more often fatally failing to do so. We have stopped to assist this risky terrapin migration many times, especially when the kids were small. We adults, unfortunately, have become resigned to the fact that some turtles, like some humans, will get hit by one tragedy or another in intercourse with the high-speed world.

In the misty rain, this turtle's wet shell glistened like a dome of enameled stone. But what struck me most about this creature was its odd markings—some kind of ancient runes. Surely there was a message here. I felt certain these symbols contained a cryptic message that might divulge the answers to Life, The Universe, and Everything. Yet, all I was able to understand of these hieroglyphs upon brief field examination was the mysterious "3." Was this turtle put here, like the illustrative plaque on Pioneer 10, to bear a message from another reality? This alien life form, I felt certain, must be examined back at home base, contemplated carefully, out of the rain. And so I prepared to take this specimen back to the mothership for closer study.

In dream-like passage, four clawed, scaly legs swam rhythmically in air. The golden turtle was borne to another world, abducted out of the realm of mosses and leaf mold by an enormous grappling five-hooked appendage. And at a terrible height of a 50-story turtle building, at terrapin mach-8 across leagues and parsecs of space— more than could be covered in a turtle lifetime—she was carried away.

At length, the rains stopped and the sun peeked briefly through the veil of Isidore's vast swirling robes of rain. The turtle hieroglyphs were recorded for further rumination. It should be mentioned that, in the varied attempts to communicate with the abducted turtle, it was finally concluded that turtles do indeed speak telepathically, but only when attaining full and sustained eye contact with the listener at close range. It is a current hypothesis that turtle thought contains the same message as John Cage's 4′33″ of silence. Listen closely. There is much to learn.

Of Life and Death and Compost

Back when I was teaching, on the first day of Biology 101, I would give a pop test. Take out a sheet of paper (can you feel the prickly sensation in your arm pits?) and write the answer to this one question: WHAT IS LIFE?

Sample Answers: Life is living. Things that are alive. (Well, yes, use the question as the answer. Nice try.) Living things breathe and move; something that is alive eats and reproduces; life is something that when its not there, its dead. And so on.

The answers I read on that sweaty sheet of paper told me what living things do: extract energy from their environment, grow, reproduce, respond to stimuli and so on—all true statements. But this is not a satisfying or complete answer. The truth is, we don't really have a definition or an equation for what life IS. We can detect it in matter by the processes we observe; we can take it away from creatures that possess it, but we cannot define it. Humility and respect for this mystery seemed a good and healthy way to begin our exploration of biology, the study of life.

If I were taking my own pop quiz, I might answer with this response, also a partial answer: life is what keeps things from being reduced to mold and ash prematurely. From rotting; decomposing; returning to dust. From premature fatal infection, infestation and microbial ingestion. This also is true, without being a full explanation, and is another thing "life" does for matter that has it.

The nature of living things is such that there are attempts to take us apart bit by bit from inside and out as soon as we—worm or mouse or leaf—are conceived. The checks and balances of the nature of life somehow equip us life-bearers to thwart most of these attempts. The ones that succeed, we call disease, infection, mycosis and such. It's a wonder we seldom consider: that life is a property of matter, a self-sustaining order against the onslaught of disorder, that keeps us more or less unconsumed from birth to death.

The instant of death is like the opening doors at the back-to-school sale at WallyWorld. Our lifeless corpse and former corpus is swarmed, permeated, and encor-porated by other corpuscles—fungi and bacteria, mostly. They pick us up by the armload and carry our material frames away. Our deconstruction begins, the recycling of all that matter that "lived" and was us. The same fate waits for the million million leaves that swirl over the top of my roof this moment, passing from tree to air to soil to mold.

Insect Epistemology

All last month as I drove the back roads of Floyd County or walked along our pasture road, I had my eye out for the first monarch of the year, but saw not a one. Now it is October, and I was about to think this would be the first year in my adult life not to see them pass down the long ridges of the southern Appalachians in autumn. They have been under some pressure throughout their range and are in danger as a species. It was sad to think that during what remains of my lifetime, the world might lose yet another familiar creature from its shrinking menagerie.

Then yesterday, a pair of wings sailed quickly by while I was raking the driveway—wings the very color of the orange maple leaves underfoot. I wasn't sure at first, but then the wings settled for a moment on the chrysanthemums near the back door. I was certain—this was my first Monarch of the year, at last. While the swallowtails by this time were tattered and pale, this butterfly had obviously hatched close by, a new floor model, low mileage, spotless and sleek and full of pep.

This male, told by the spot and thinner veins on the wings, was full of himself, expending more energy than was wise for one who still had an enormously long late autumn voyage ahead. It was skittish and flitty as I approached with my camera for a portrait. I moved in close for a tight shot. But just when I touched the shutter, off he flap-flap-flaped in a large erratic circle, flying as far as the barn across the creek. He is out earning his learner's permit on new wings and may be about to leave the neighborhood for good, I thought. But he always came back to the big cluster of pale orange mums. The flowers, opened for only a day, were as pristine and unblemished as this brand new butterfly.

I confess that I had never really noted the very different pattern of flight the monarch displays compared to the spicebush swallowtails and fritillaries that have been so common around here all summer. The Monarch pattern is very definitely flap-flap-G L I D E. And this passive gliding makes sense when I consider that a butterfly born on the East Coast is destined to winter more than two thousand miles to the southwest.

If the monarch did not know how to glide on the supportive and propulsive air, it would never be capable of its winter vacation (and death) in central Mexico each year. If it could not glide, it would not be able to rise in the thermals and coast effortlessly for miles, heading south and west. Watching this butterfly soar, I remembered that I used to know how to fold a piece of wide-ruled school paper to make a glider airplane that would have amazing hang-time, almost floating on the air. It is that bit of aerodynamics that the monarch knows.

Like an eagle, no heavier than a feather, it knows how to adjust its wings and modify its flight path to air currents over vast distances with little effort by gliding and soaring on the thermals. Like a warbler, the monarch knows how to orient to the invisible pull of unknown energies or to landmarks in the sky, or on or under earth, It knows how to migrate over unfamiliar thousands of miles to a place it has never been before. Monarchs know how to feed on the sticky sap of milkweed that makes them unsavory food for would-be predators, insuring that at least some survive long enough to sail away to the West to take a long nap with hundreds of thousands of their kind. All of this they somehow know.

What they know about buoyancy and loft, about milkweed toxins and about the geography of the continent is hardwired, ordained, immutable and the same from one butterfly to its offspring—truth unchanging through an infinite procession of a thousand generations. A monarch, with its tiny speck of brain simply knows that it knows what it knows and that is enough. These orange and black wisps of will know where they're going and how to get there, born with Heaven in their wiring and their wings.

Vegetable Horrors

The asparagus of childhood appears in memory like dead green fingers from a cold can, and I can clearly see its gray green squishiness lying there limp and dead on the plate. The thought evokes the buttery burning rubber smell of it and soon I feel the familiar rising tightness moving up my throat—even now, half a century later—and I approach the very edge of emetic crisis. The sight, smell, the very thought of asparagus used to make my digestive system go into violent reverse peristaltic waves and all was lost.

My parents claimed this was a vegetable. To my mind, this vile substance was never anything more than a green poison created by children-loathing adults on the other side of the Iron Curtain. That is where, in those days, the Evil Ones lived. And THEY must be responsible for this. I hated them, and I loathed the mind control they exerted over my parents to make them insist that, to become or to remain amongst the "good children", this toxic substance must go in, go down and stay down. This of course was not humanly possible, and the enemy thus exerted a hegemonic form of psychic tyranny over adult and child alike. Those were terrible times.

Many years later, having escaped the Gulag of Childhood, I found myself the new owner of twenty acres of sunlight and rich earth. I was enjoying—yes enjoying—cutting our acre of grass for the first time with the push mower in early spring. There in a flat area that I assumed was a flower bed, a thin, pale, green and shiny stalk had pushed through the leaf litter. Its top was faintly adorned with small overlapping artichoke-like leaves on a frail and tapering tip. This was asparagus. I recognized it from the wanted posters I had seen as a child.

I had learned in my botanizing that this stuff grew wild, and was even stalked by those who also thought many parts of a picnic table were edible. Wild Asparagus was to die for, according to some brainwashed and pitiful souls. Here in my new yard it apparently grew as an act of intention—all the more awful and repugnant, I thought as I mowed up and down, coming closer and closer to the dreaded plant with each pass. But alas, I was lured to it like a tongue to a frozen pump handle in winter, and I plucked the awful spear from the ground. It held me in its chlorophyllic trance. I put it in my mouth. What was I doing!?

I ate it and it did not threaten to come back up. It was, in fact, delicious! It was at that moment that I discovered the difference between fresh and embalmed asparagus. Succulent and slightly crunchy, fresh asparagus tasted of summer sun, rich humus and all things green and growing. Such is the way with knowing there is no middle man between your food's life in the soil and your first bite of it fresh from the earth. From the time they could browse the garden rows, my children loved fresh green peas (another canned gaggy childhood horror for me) because they could pull Sugar Snaps warm from the trellis and eat them like candy.

So parents, if your vegetable-challenged children hide canned peas in their cheeks or smuggle them to the family dog; if they threaten to bring back the meal's slightly-chewed metal-entombed asparagus back onto their plates (and who can blame them?), just send them browsing to the garden. Produce fresh from the vine may forever change their little minds about those loathsome good-for-you foods that so horrified you and me as hungry but mistrusting children. (You must remember, however, that for some veggies for some people—brussel sprouts or rutabagas, for instance—there may be no redemption, no matter how fresh.)

The Green Tide Rises

It always comes and goes too fast, and I always promise myself each year I will not let it happen. Yet here I am again watching spring mature its way to the tops of mountains and roses (wild ones, and countless familiar spring weeds and wildflowers) will bloom unseen. I watch the season oozing into summer from my truck window as I drive the Great Valley east from Shawsville to Salem.

When the trees have fully leafed out in the late spring, the curtain is across the forested views. The show is not over. It just goes on behind the veil.

Leaf-out begins in the low warm valleys and creeps up the southern slopes in April. It overwhelms even the high remote ridges of southwest Virginia by mid-May. This blooming flood of leafery—oak and spicebush, tulip poplar and ironwood, sarvice, dogwood, sumac and cherry—covers the empty gray forms of winter trees, hiding branch, then limb, then trunk. And finally, when it is all done and small translucent spring leaves have grown from the size of mouse ears to their full shape and are no longer thin and transparent, we will not be able to see into the forest for the trees.

The valley floor along highway 460 in eastern Montgomery County lies a good bit lower than Goose Creek—some 1200 feet there compared to 2100 for our place here. From the Elliston Valley highway to the south towards Poor Mountain rises a series of stair-step broken ridges cresting at 1700, then 1900, 2700 and 3500 feet into the distance. The lowest gentle slopes are in mixed pasture spotted with grazing cattle that dot the grounds of venerable old plantations like Fotheringay—archetypal Virginia countryside at its loveliest. The highest range in the background some four miles distant bristles with antennae and towers, where Poor Mountain forms the western rim of the Roanoke Valley.

As the season matures, the bloom-line tide rises slowly, day by day, to leave its mark higher and higher up the mountain slopes, coming sooner and faster on the southern exposures. For all practical botanical purposes, this week it is still winter on the higher peaks that stand gaunt, brown and threadbare above a riot of green and chartreuse rising up from below. It may seem like mid-spring here already; but at the Mt. Rogers Naturalist

Rally in early May, it will only be early spring at the campgrounds at 4000 feet, and spring wildflowers will be at their peak there, but gone-by for weeks here at the house.

If you use the leafing dates of the stair-step ridges as a yardstick, our hillsides here in our deep valley are blooming and budding as if they lived at 2500 to 3000 feet instead the actual 2100. We are in a sheltered valley, a cold sink, a frost pocket—a microhabitat such that we are cooler than one would find for this elevation in general and our trees take their sweet time showing any green. Being in a cooler-than-typical locale is a problem when it comes to frosts and freezes for the garden and fruit trees; but it is not always a problem. This sweltering summer, I'll hear the forecast for southwest Virginia:

"Today in Roanoke, highs will be 80 to 85, except 5 to 10 degrees cooler for the New River Valley (where we live) and points west."

To which I will gleefully add: "And at least another 5 degrees cooler yet on Goose Creek!"

Field Notes: April

Ferns: Northern maidenhair ferns hold their most delicate and perfect symmetry in late April, gathering light in the glades before the overstory fills in completely. If God made ferns to show what he could do with a leaf, He inspired their names as poetry. When I am alone, I may say their Latin names out loud as I see them for the first time each spring—like greeting old friends. Interrupted fern; New York fern; cinnamon, Christmas, sensitive and hay-scented ferns. *Onoclea sensibilis. Thelypteris noveboracensis. Dennstaedtia punctilobula. Osmunda cinnamomea.* Welcome back!

Mayapple: I have my own personal way of measuring the seasons. The arrival of the spiders that spin their webs across our path marks mid-summer. Earlier in the year, to mark mid-spring, the blooming of mayapple is the key. Their wadded twists of leaves appear almost overnight in early May, and when it is officially mid-spring on Goose Creek, the mayapple will bear the single waxy white flower hidden underneath.

Spring Rains: With all the rain this spring, the pasture grass has grown rangy, tall and supple. It bends gracefully with the breezes, green blades bowing in unison in swirls and swaths, like the green coat of a sunning beast stroked by a great invisible hand.

Morels: Found this morning: three morel mushrooms by accident—enough to provide the suggestion of earthiness to the stroganoff tonight. Three more would have been better. On the intentional foray this afternoon with bag in hand, I am convinced that mushrooms disguised themselves and became invisible. Hint for next year: Never carry a collecting bag where the morels can see it.

Blackberries: It is looking like a good berry year ahead, up on the logged land behind the house. The ravaged forest is coming back now in lithe, fast-growing white pines and many, many berries. We've already notified some friends that they are welcome to come pick as much as they want later this summer. Bring your own buckets, we told them. We'll provide the berries, the scratches and the ticks.

Wild Strawberries: We've lived here long enough now we know not to expect to harvest many of the wild strawberries. Covering the old postal road up the valley, their white flower petals lie scattered underfoot like confetti the day after an outdoor wedding. We'll get none of the little red fruits. The turkeys and grouse, chipmunks and groundhogs—and I think especially the box turtles—will gobble them up even while the berries are still green. Life is not always fair when it comes to wild fruit.

Bird sounds: Today, the first scarlet tanager, heard but not seen. As usual, he called from somewhere in the uppermost branches where the indigo buntings also prefer to perch and sing. Great crested flycatchers' buzzy calls are coming from the big walnuts over by the barn. The "pleased-to-meetcha Missus Beecha" that the bird books describe, I still cannot hear in the song of the chestnut-sided warblers.

Hemlocks: Sadly, we've not yet seen the first black throated blue warblers this year, and I'm afraid they will become more and more uncommon as our once magnificent darkest green hemlock trees succumb to the insect called the wooly adelgid. Our hillsides were once covered with the black-green fronds of hemlock—my favorite tree. Now they stand gaunt and gray, sad skeletons with boney arms uplifted, frozen in a final unanswered prayer.

Fireflies: Last night late, we saw the first flashes in ones and twos—the earliest fireflies just practicing for the Hallelujah Chorus of Fireflies that will come in legions by late June. I close my eyes and see, in memory of summers past, a constellation of pulsing yellow-golden lights. They will come down to earth on a June night when we can smell the warm meadow in the dark, and we will see in the distance, at the edge of vision, silent flashes of summer lightning.

I Can't See Clearly Now

A thousand years ago on a day in May, a Cherokee hunter surveyed the skyline from the top of the Floyd County mountain peak we now call Rocky Knob. When a cold front slid down from Canada, the weather for a few days would remain clear and spring-crisp. He could clearly see Walker Mountain on the skyline thirty miles northwest, sharp and blue against the brilliant cerulean sky. Later in the spring and summer of a thousand years ago, the ridges would have appeared smudged and fading into the distance, blues softened and edges blunted by a diaphanous vapor of plant breath—what scientists now call transpirational water vapor. It rose in clouds from the wooded valleys, a product of photosynthesis from the sea of broadleaved trees in the Appalachian Forest— denser then, by far, than our cut-over forests of today. For eons, our ridges have been naturally blue, our mountains smoky from a billion breathing leaves.

We've just had a wonderful gift of cool, clear air pass through this week, and the world has edges again after a bleary, humid spell. As this giant air mass moves on, plant vapor will accumulate and the distant ridges will grow blue and smoky. A few days later and for much of the summer, those landmarks two or three miles away and beyond will remain hazy in a blue-gray photochemical smog. The two million visitors that travel the Blue Ridge Parkway on the edge of Floyd County every year will, for months, see only the smoggy ridge top they are driving on and little more beyond. This is an aesthetic tragedy to be sure. But more than that, when I consider all that I cannot see in the acidic air, it brings to mind the real tragedy: this tainted air is causing massive, forever damage in the southern forest. It will cost us to clean up our air. It is already costing us not to.

Gardening Hopefully

Through decades of gardening expectations and delusion, I have come to understand this: the terms fusarium resistant, slow-bolt, early-bearing, long-standing, high-yielding and such are just fortune cookie fantasies told on the backs of fairy tale seed packets. Your mileage will vary. No matter the scientific advances your seeds are said to possess, or the drastic and creative measures you might take to outsmart or appease the gardening demons and gods, you and your vegetables are totally subject to the vagaries of continent-sized wet or dry, hot or cold masses of mindless air that sometimes favor and sometimes punish. The rains will fall and the wilting sun will scorch the godly and the ungodly alike.

Yet knowing this, I can already see this year's garden in my hopes as it might grow to be. I stand here watching my seeds deluged by the rains of early June, and I am prepared for those thrills and agonies that will come. But I know this: when it gets right down to it, chance, more often than not, will trump a gardener's best design.

Still, in spite of the uncertainties and risks, some of the fruits of our labor will end up in colorful rows on our cellar shelves where full Mason jars bear testimony to this gardening year's good luck and God's blessing, a dash of chance and a pinch of miracle, and enough but not too much rain.

Homeland Defense

With the warmer weather, enemy forces are mobilizing and have already established fortified positions around our headquarters here on Goose Creek—under the eaves, over the front door, even within the very substance of the house itself. The time has come to carry out the counter-attack. Danger lurks. Wish us luck.

We had supper on the front porch for the first time last night. Ah, the sounds of the creek, the gentle breeze as the warm sun slants across the meadow, the dog flopped out in front of us waiting a morsel from our plates when we're done. All was right with the world and we sat contentedly, surveying with satisfaction all the changes we'd made in the old place in just a few years. And then, we glanced up and YUK! that Danged Phoebe had piled moss and mud and poop on the lintel plate over the front door again! Black slime oozed down the white clapboards in a most unappetizing way. Now phoebes are good birds to have around, being insectivores and all. But the little cow pie over the door had to go.

Meanwhile, as we cursed the bird nest, we discovered that the paper wasps had made a front door to their hive through the tiniest of slits under the edge of the front porch roof where I hadn't caulked completely. They flew around us clumsily, bumping the backs of our heads solely for the purpose of aggravation, while we attempted to enjoy our first-of-the-season outdoor meal. Shopping list: latex caulk and a case of wasp spray. Oh, and I must have missed spraying that little strip of foundation at the corner of the porch because there is a motorcade of carpenter ants going up the downspout. I think I hear them singing a little marching song—or maybe I've just seen one too many Pixar animations.

And from our perch on the porch with our dinner plates, we see that the hot pink bleeding hearts are in full glory, bobbing gently in the late afternoon breeze. They are being buzzily pollinated by—wait! Those look like carpenter bees! "Hey Ann, do you remember how Nate and I used to do battle with the carpenter bees? Hold on a minute. I'll be back." I ran upstairs to The Very Back Room.

The grip on my old Wilson STING racquet feels familiar, even though it has sat idle now for six years. I rotate it just so in my grip, test the full swing of it a time or two, and I am ready. This one looks like a male. He'll be ornery. There's a swing-and-a-miss. Now he's really riled—buzzing madly, saying vile curses in bee language, flying back and forth, back and forth in a predictable aggressive pattern. Aha! one more zig and on the zag—PING! Service ace. The thrill of victory. The agony of defeat. This is biological control at its most satisfying best, even knowing that while I win this battle, we are losing the war.

Or Would you Rather be a Cow?

My children have spent a lifetime embarrassed because their daddy drives the speed limit—or slower, especially on the back roads and particularly when wildflowers bloom, birds flitter or the sky is blue, or a string of sixties tunes is transporting me to a distant age and a younger, simpler, slower incarnation in this life. I'm used to having people sniffing my exhaust and heck no I won't pull over and let them pass. I'm going the blinking speed limit. Almost.

And I'm as slow as January molasses on our walks around here, with the emphasis on the journey, not the destination. (I should mention that I am married to a race horse mostly interested in the finish line.) Like a cow, I can be happy standing in the same place, staring at the ground for hours. The grass is greener right there where I am, by golly, and I can stay contentedly in that one place and watch it grow.

Cows know what to expect for the day ahead because they read the signs. Watch them find their place in the pasture in anticipation of coming rain: poor man's weathervane, they call them. I am aware of the shift in winds to the east and know when snow or rain is coming; I smell ozone before the storm gets here; and I know where to go to find shade at any time of any day, to shelter from the wind, and from worry, and Ann says—from work. And I can lie down and nap in a heartbeat. And although you will rarely see a living cow lying on its back, barrel belly to the sky, that's the way I like it—a world of solid ground beneath me, infinity above me forever, a supplicant cow-man; a spinning, orbiting, expanding cosmic bovine speck.

And so on the way to town today, I drove slowly, of course, contemplating the cattle on a thousand hills, as well as the soft green hills themselves. I ate dinner slowly with a friend in town, then settled down in a deep wallow of a chair at the local library with a good book. And on the way home this afternoon, I marveled at the variety of roadside weeds that I have learned never again to take as common. It is these tatters of white and blue and yellow that I so missed along the busy edges of places I have lived away from here during years when Southwest Virginia seemed like a greener but galactically far-off pasture.

I savor their names like old wine. Chickory: *Chicorium intybus*—a binomial rhythm that always makes me think of a Druid incantation, a hex on a jilting lover, perhaps. Sweet clovers: yellow and white— *Melilothus*. And *Asclepius*: common milkweed named after an ancient Greek physician, his commemorative genus buzzing along our pasture's edge now with red milkweed beetles and skipper moths. Milkweed visitors soon will include the monarch butterfly extracting poisons from the milky sap. Rhododendrons bloom white and pink where there is enough sunlight through the cool forest shade overhead to coax them into blossom.

These untidy random volunteers planted by no one in God's garden make me smile. Rounding a bend in the road and coming upon familiar friends is to find a common thread of memory from all the pastures I have grazed in among these Blue Ridges, and on other roads on so many journeys. I know what to expect of these particular bends, and it is comforting. This is familiar country to me now, after seven years in Floyd County, more than four years in this house, and countless hours standing enthralled, cow-like in our pasture or woods, or embedded to mid-calf in the cold creek. I am bovine in my ways, happiest to be out standing in my field chewing my cud, and up to my knees in flowers.

Part Three:
Roads Remembered

Finding Our Place

My mother never lived anywhere but town and always said wistfully that she was born with "country" in her blood. I was born with the mountains in mine.

I know I looked foolish in an Eddie Bauer down jacket that balmy Birmingham October night, sitting on the steps in front of our southside apartment. The year was 1974. Soon, I'd be going where the weather suited my clothes, and I had already left my native Alabama in my mind.

That down parka on a too-warm southern night was a vestment of possibility, and it wrapped me in our future.

That hour began the metamorphosis of new belonging from past to future; from south to north. In the streetlight glow of my home town, I traveled hopefully ahead to December when we would pack and go, to real winters, to the high places of southwest Virginia. There would be wonderful darkness there and our children would know the constellations. We would hear the winds of real northern winters blowing and see clear creeks flowing. Hope carried me far beyond the exhaust fumes in the heart of the city, and I could smell the sweet air of those mountain realms where we'd be moving soon. Ann and I and our infant daughter were bound for Virginia and for our future. It had called to us, and we had answered. I was leaving home to find it.

It was snowing when we arrived in Wytheville towing our few belongings in the U-Haul; and I was wearing my down parka. We stayed there twelve years, and they were good years for us, mostly. We had a constant group of friends and lifelong jobs if we wanted them. I taught in the biology department at the community college and Ann was a pharmacist at the local hospital. Our kids were happy there. We had acquired a familiarity with the lay of the land and had a clear sense of our place in it. Soon we moved to our first little farm on Greasy Creek outside town and things were good. Maybe they were too good, too easy. We sold the farm in 1987 and moved our belongings back to Birmingham. But our hearts never stopped belonging in Virginia.

We stayed in Alabama long enough for me to replace my old career in teaching with my new one in physical therapy—no small ordeal for a man almost forty. With a physical therapist license, we could make our home most anywhere in the country that we wanted. We chose Asheville as the center of our search, and spent two years in Sylva, North Carolina at the gateway to the Smokies, then seven in Morganton, in the shadow of Grandfather Mountain. It seemed I could find work and live anywhere now—but only as long as there were mountains in view.

After all that time as Tarheels, as our children began to fledge, we were seduced by the invisible forces of belonging that never stopped pulling us back to Virginia. Ann imagined a white farmhouse waiting for us there—"a house with double porches and a creek nearby" she dreamed out loud. We longed for roots, and the mountains of Carolina were beautiful. But they didn't hold the soil where we were meant to grow in the autumn of our lives. Virginia's mountains did.

When we made our first exploratory trip to Floyd County early in 1996, we knew nothing about it beyond what one can see from looking at a map. It lies within the Blue Ridge mountain range and stands on a plateau that falls off sharply on its northeast end toward Roanoke. It drops even more sharply down the escarpment south and east of the Blue Ridge Parkway that forms the county's entire southern border. There is no national forest in the county. There are no airports, no interstates, few villages and one major intersection and a single traffic light in the town of Floyd, population 400. The odds weren't good we'd find work there; and what about entertainment, or culture, or community in a place so out-of-the-way?

And so it was no small surprise in early July of '97 to be living alone in a cabin on Walnut Knob, just off the Parkway about a dozen miles from the traffic light in Floyd. I would be managing a physical therapy outpatient clinic in town. Across the street from the clinic was the Country Store—long-time home of the Friday Night Jamboree. I could see Ralph the barber cutting hair, or playing the guitar with the boys if things were slow, over in the barbershop no more than a hundred feet from that single traffic light. Now, we had established our relocation base camp back in Virginia. We had pitched our tent here (or at least I had) but it would take an eagle to give us hope that we'd find in Floyd the permanent home we had been longing for all our years together.

In February 1999—the month the PT clinic that had brought me here closed down—we signed a contract on some remote mountain land and a very old house on Goose Creek. In March (for Ann's birthday) we found our second Virginia black lab pup, Buster. He went with us every trip, back and forth between our cabin on the Parkway and the old home place we would soon be restoring. And in May, we began six months of work on this century-old farmhouse in the can't-get-here-from-there northeast corner of the county. We undertook the work with a growing confidence that every improvement was an investment in our future here that would last the rest of our days.

First, a new foundation went down into bedrock—an under-girding for the long haul, a new stability in our lives; then, a new front porch rose up on the sunny south side—a welcoming invitation to sit and talk. New windows filled the dark spaces inside with new light. Two woodstoves brought the promise of warm winter nights by the fire. Wiring and indoor plumbing gave us all the modern conveniences. And from within this solid old house built very nearly the year that the telephone was invented, I would have an internet connection to the larger world—a lifeline that would become my thread of contact with the world outside of Goose Creek.

By November, the workmen had made a couple of rooms livable for us and we moved from Walnut Knob. Here was Ann's white farmhouse with double porches, a dream come true. She wanted to give the place a name. She called it "Here's Home." I hoped that she was right.

In May, 2001, I went back into full-time work as therapist-manager in a clinic in Christiansburg, a half-hour drive north. Ann was secure in her job at a hospital in Salem near Roanoke. We seemed about to reach that blessed state on the back-nine of our lives and careers—that place where you finally think you should be able to lower your vigilance, unclench your jaws, take slow easy breaths thinking you have earned the right to slow down, to just be present in the moment, arrived at last.

But when things seem too good to last, they probably won't. Sure enough, exactly one year later in May 2002, things fell apart. It seemed like a good time to step away from career and duty and get my personal bearings. Turns out, looking back, that it was a most providential disaster.

Work: It Happens

I watch the world of work as an outsider these days. I'll dive back in, if the right job comes along. But by the time you reach my age, you know that no matter how good a job looks before you start it, there will be days when you'll need hip waders for mucking around in the barnyard bog most jobs eventually become. I remember when Nathan was five years old, a precocious reader, and eagerly vocal in large groups. He understood what I'm saying here about the "w" word. Let me explain.

We were gathered for a meal on the eve of the relocation of a friend and co-worker of mine from the community college. A dozen or so friends of the soon-to-be former associate were coming to the end of our last meal together at the Chinese Restaurant in Wytheville. It was time for the fortune cookies.

We went around the table reading our predictable mock-Confucian fortunes—you know the routine. The reading came round the table to young Nathan, who insisted that he would take his turn by himself, and no help here, thank you. He started out with relative ease:

"Your....wor...working....life....will be...fi....filled..."

With furrowed brow, he paused briefly. He was stumped by a word he didn't know, but we had worked some with him on phonics (although he was not hooked) and he was determined to make a stab at it. By this time, the entire restaurant crowd was silently listening, marveling at the early reading skills and general pluckiness of this extroverted, fat-cheeked little chap.

"Your working life will be filled...with... (and he completed the sentence loudly in triumph) ... EXCREMENT!"

Everybody in the place cracked up! A few spewed chow mien across their tables. We could hardly catch our breath! It was just too perfect—and was even funnier when we reached over and read that his cookie fortune actually ended with the word EXCITEMENT! Way to go, Nate. You were wise before your time. Out of the mouths of babes.

Chickens Come Home to Roost

Our young, world-traveling son was home for a short visit this past week. My daughter and granddaughter were with us last month. It's wonderful having our children with us again, but when they come home to visit, it hints of victims returning to the scene of the crime. They bring with them a remembered list of offenses long past, holding parental felons to account for ancient crimes. Our son and daughter will eventually get around to a good-natured rubbing of our noses in past parenting offenses and misdemeanors. They are not quite ready to let us—or themselves—forget.

Nathan discovered "Urban Legends of Childhood" lying on my desk. This was something I'd written recently for the weblog about fantastic and often scary things that little kids hear from their older peers. It also described the tiny white lies of coercion that children are sometimes told by mind-molding, well-intentioned parents. It seems my fatherly transgressions are doomed to come back to haunt me through my children, and Nathan, reading my story, was quick to remind me once more of one particular incident that has become a legend of sorts in our own family.

We had just moved from the town of Wytheville to our little farm in the nearby countryside and were enjoying a beautiful early summer afternoon out on the deck. Three year old Nathan was reveling in an unrestrained barefoot frenzy of activity in his new country back yard. On this warm July day under towering white clouds that moved silently overhead like great ships, Nathan chased cats and climbed in the boxwoods that grew beside the driveway. He hunted in the clover for bumblebees. Finding one, he would crouch on his knees in the grass and stroke the furry black and yellow insect with his chubby little finger. "They won't hurt me! They're my friends" he explained. His faith in the goodness of nature and man was quite remarkable. And you know, his friends, the bumblebees never once stung him, but those that loved him did, ever so slightly, with a small deceit.

"Nathan!" I called from the deck, and he came running on his stumpy little legs. "Nathan, did you know that if you flap your arms up and down, up and down, really, really fast, you can fly?!"

His eyes went wide as hen eggs and straightway he leapt off the two steps from the deck into the grassy yard and commenced to rev his engines and strive for altitude. We watched transfixed from our lawn chairs. Without a trace of doubt, his legs and arms churned the air as he ran back and forth under the old apple tree. "Faster! FASTER!" we exhorted, amazed at his sincerity and persistence. Back and forth he went, up the hill and down. At last, he collapsed with his wings and landing gear totally failed. Onlookers at the airport were quick to praise him. "You darn near made it, boy. I thought there for a minute you were about to head off over the barn!"

Our son reminds me of this fatherly crime rather often. And I don't know exactly how guilty he wants me to feel about having told him this parental fairy tale, this little bit of trickery and magic on a summer afternoon long ago. I do know that for an instant, he was convinced that he could fly. And somehow, I don't think that belief and expectation ever quite left him. Both of our children have grown wings since those days. They have taken great leaps into the unknown, and remained aloft in a most graceful kind of flight. And now I wonder, when their time comes, and their stocky little 3-year-old runs barefoot in the yard on a summer day—will they tell her she can fly? I do hope so.

Like a Dog

The first summer after we moved to Virginia as young, naïve adults, my mother Betty Jean and grandmother Bea made the long drive up from Alabama to see us in our new home—a rambling, drafty old house on a tree-lined street in what seemed like a very small town, moving there from busy Birmingham. I had told my family visitors of the kindness of our neighbors, Euell and his wife, who had shared produce with us from their garden and honey from Euell's hives. He had even given us firewood in the early months when we were so cold and clueless in our adopted rural lifestyle.

When he found out my relatives were coming to visit, our good neighbor asked if I thought they might like to take a drive out to the cove where he managed several hundred acres of magnificent valley pasture and rolling woodlands. We could take his big truck up into the logging roads where he and I often cut firewood together. I thought my visitors would enjoy that, so a day or two after they arrived, we made plans to take an afternoon excursion. My grandmother declined the invitation but insisted that mom, Ann and I go on ahead with Euell to the country. Bea stood in the shade of our large wrap-around front porch and watched us drive away—Euell and Jill, his black spaniel dog, in his flatbed truck, with the rest of us driving out to the cove in my car.

We returned a few hours later having spent a very nice afternoon in the woods and on the county roads, all of us crammed into the cabin of my neighbor's one-ton flat-bed truck. Of course right away when we got home, my grandmother wanted to know all about it. Mom was gushing with adjectives to describe how majestic the mountains were, praising the clouds and the wildflowers, everything we had seen. She described our afternoon adventure to Bea in typical superlatives.

"When we got out to the farm, Freddie and Ann and I got in the truck with Euell and drove way back in the woods. It was just wonderful!" she exclaimed.

"Well" Bea asked "what did Jill do?"

"Oh, there wasn't room in the cab for all of us, so Euell made her get out and run along behind the truck."

Bea seemed visibly disturbed by this, but being the genteel southern lady she was, she couched her disapproval in the mildest of negatives. "Well, I don't think that was a very nice thing to do" she scolded.

We didn't see what was so disturbing about this, but tried to assure her it was nothing out of the ordinary.

"Oh, its okay. Euell always makes her get out and run when they go out to the cove. She needs the exercise" I explained.

You could see the indignation rise in my grandmother's countenance as she said "Now Betty, it's just not right that you should come up here a visitor and cause a man to make his wife get out and run along behind the truck!"

In a simultaneous flash of comprehension, we understood my grandmother's confusion. As we laughed harder, Bea grew more and more perplexed and more disgusted with our insensitivity to the treatment of Euell's wife. When finally we could catch our breath, we told her "Bea, Jill is the dog!"

"Oh, she said "I thought that was his wife. When you drove off today, didn't I see her sitting in the truck next to Euell?"

Because her confusion was now understandable it was no less hilarious. Looking into the cab of the truck from behind, sure enough, Jill did look for all the world like a straight-haired brunette sitting there on the truck seat snuggled up extra-close to our neighbor.

Years later, Ann and I would watch the two of them, man and dog, sitting side by side, spouse-like in Euell's truck as they drove out to the country to tend the cattle.

"There they go again" we'd say. "You know, one of these days, Jill will have had it with running behind the truck and she'll show up over at the Humane Society to file for divorce!"

Easy Going Down

My daughter, Holli and a friend once conspired to pull a fast one on unsuspecting daddy. They cut out some giggly pink-brown cookie-shaped patties of Play Dough and baked them in their Easy Bake Oven. There was a plot afoot.

I looked up from my reading as the girls came tumbling into the room, falling over themselves to offer me the "cookies." They were about to pee their pants with anticipation, so I prolonged the suspense.

"Hmmmm! These look really good! Did you girls bake them yourselves? Maybe I should save this for later."

"No daddy, go ahead and eat them now" they chortled, barely able to contain their conspiratorial glee. I got up from the Lazy Boy and fetched a glass of milk from the refrigerator, and came back to nestle into a comfortable cookie-eating position. I took up the whole mess of cookies and held them greedily, commending the girls on their efforts and telling them "I'm so hungry I think I could eat every one of these right now!" knowing they expected me to realize they were not REAL cookies and end the game right there.

I took the first cookie, stuffed the whole thing in my mouth, chewed heartily, and swallowed. The horror! The horror! Their eyeballs bulged as they looked at each other in disbelief.

"Daddy, those were not real cookies! They're Play Dough! Don't eat it! Spit it out!" The guilt of a trick too well executed overwhelmed them.

I burped violently, and then I began to shake, bug-eyed, staring blankly into the distance. There was a pregnant moment when they were not sure if I was about to croak, or was just jerking them around, as I had been known to do on more than one occasion in their short past. I never did tell them that I almost yakked getting the dang thing down; but I was determined to show them that the one being tricked can sometimes become the trickster.

My grown daughter has never forgotten this little prank, nor have I. If my granddaughter pulls the same stunt on me as her mother did and offers me a pink mock-cookie, I've decided in advance that one Play Dough cookie per lifetime is my limit.

Labrador Tractor Abatement Policy

Our neighbor was over today with his tractor to pick up a few round bales of hay he'd left back behind the barn. Buster didn't even bother lifting his head to see what the commotion was all about. But I remembered a time that tractor noises sent everybody in our family running to hold back our first black lab, Zachary, before he got us all in trouble. Again.

Yes, Buster is our second pure-bred Black Labrador Retriever. If you've ever been around Black Labs you know that they have probably the best temperament of any large dog. (I have no idea that this is gospel truth, but have no experience to the contrary.) And being pure-bred, you might expect considerable consistency of character down a lineage and in the breed in general. Now, Zachary and Buster did share the common features of being broad of chest, and black, but at that point, the similarities pretty much end.

Buster here, we have concluded, has a distinctive home-schooled quality. He is totally trusting, awkwardly sociable with strangers, polite and never pushy. He doesn't bark, doesn't chew up things, and is remarkably naive about life in general. He doesn't tolerate change very well, or grasses touching his undercarriage. He is most comfortable sitting in his place on the back porch, and when he comes up missing on a walk, you can pretty much know that he has already made his way home. He will be curled up in front of the door waiting for you by the time you return.

Zachary, on the other hand, was more reform-schooled—gentle with the kids and intelligent, but headstrong. He was fully aware of how intimidating and formidable he was, and when a stranger drove up in the yard, Zach would charge at full speed, menacingly heisted up on his front legs with a line down his back and teeth bared. The visitor stayed in the car until we called the dog back to the house. If it was a salesman of some sort—especially any form of insurance—we apologized that we were sorry but we couldn't do anything with the dog and maybe he or she had better not roll down his windows very far; and more often than not, they would just leave. He was a handy dog to have around. But Zach chewed up, barked, and ran off frequently to who-knows-where and came back when he got good and danged ready.

When we belonged to Zach many years ago, there was an old farm across the dirt road from our first little farm on Greasy Creek, just off the old Wilderness Road in Wythe County. Other than pasture, only a collapsed farmhouse and a few decrepit outbuildings dotted the slant of pasture. This particular country person who owned the place came from time to time to tend the field corn planted there. For reasons which we never understood, Zachary could not abide that fellow, and the grizzly old farmer was likewise terrified of Zach. We wouldn't even realize that the man was over there until we heard his high-pitched, squeaky voice hollering at the dog to "G'on! Git away from me!" This made the dog all the bolder. Terrorizing the old farmer became Zachary's favorite sport.

One day, the farmer had slipped in across the way and was walking around in the new furrows when the dog spied his tractor through the hedge. Zach was off like a shot. The old coot saw him coming and ran in a panic for his tractor idling nearby, shrieking at the top of his shrill voice and flailing his skinny arms as he ran. He mounted that tractor in a bound and hit the throttle and sped off, opposite the direction of the dog, who was bearing down fast upon him.

Seems that there was one little problem, though. The terrified farmer had forgotten that the plow blade was sunk deep in the soil, and as he made his panicky zigzag getaway, a two-foot-thick rope of clay and grass was laid up like a wavy snake of sod all the way back to the old barn, as Zachary, the reform-school dog, closed the distance. It was one of the funniest sights I had witnessed in my short life of country living—like an episode of Dukes of Hazzard, for certain.

This was all quite funny around the dinner table that night, until the phone rang. It was the geezer, telling me in his strident, rusty-hinged voice about how my dog had made him rurn his pasture, and it was my responsibility to make it right, by gawd.

So, every afternoon for the next week, I rolled that clay rope of fescue and orchard grass back into its furrow, sweating and cussing that dog, but chuckling as I thought what a great memory this was going to be some day, after the blisters on my hands had healed.

Yes, Zachary was his own dog, and there was nothing could be done about that. Now, on the other hand, had Buster seen our farmer and his tractor across the road, he would have gone over and introduced himself. Politely, he would have asked the man if he could watch the plow-ing because in his home schooling, he was doing a unit about farmers and farming, and he would promise not to get in the way, please sir. And he could not stay long, because he really needed to get back to his post up there on the front porch, thank you kindly.

On Eagle Wings

There are a few days like this in late October when the air is clean, the sky is far-away blue and a few crisp yellow leaves still cling to the top of a tulip poplar here and there—ragged pinafores that remain along the rim of hills around us. Such days are made for the scrapbook of seasons—perfect samples of fall—so we will not forget in mid-January how good life has been in this cold valley.

This is a good day to be in a high place. Ridge views are everywhere from the high ground that envelops us, but to reach them, we must climb. The north ridge begins just outside our back door. Two hundred feet beyond the edge of the yard we stand seventy feet above the metal roof, looking down on a toy version of our white farmhouse. A fine blue-white wisp of smoke connects the chimney with the clear air above. A few hundred yards farther still and we are by then so high that the full arc of valley opens below us. Gasping for breath, we look out on the tops of ridges beyond, waiting like waves about to break. The gravel road is a thin, gray line snaking between the pines. Here and there the bright reflection of the water flickers through the spicebush and alders that have grown up through the old rock wall along Nameless

Creek. We hear the rise and fall of voices from the riffles of the cold creek below and far away.

❧

It was late October, 1997—a time in our lives not destined to become a scrap of pleasant memory for our book of days. I was living alone in a small cabin on Walnut Knob, just off the Blue Ridge Parkway, thirteen miles from Floyd where I had just begun work. On a clear day after almost all the leaves had fallen, fifty-mile views opened in three directions from that high peninsula of land that fingered out into the piedmont, gently rumpled a thousand feet below. Clear days at the cabin were spectacular but rare in the early fall of my new life alone. For days, weeks on end, the cold fog rose up from the wet lowlands and roosted in the bare trees along the escarpment—a wet brooding shroud of muted grayness and silence. Fog pressed farther and farther down into my own thoughts, cut me off from sight and sound, from place and the passing of time.

I had no choice but to be there in the fog in no one's company but my own. Ann and I had decided that, should a job in my field be offered me here in Floyd County, I would take it. We had been away from the mountains for ten years, and it was time to return and settle down for good. But Ann was halfway through a degree then and wouldn't be able to join me for a year. We would see each other on weekends, occasionally. Putting roots down in southwest Virginia was our priority, now that the kids were out of the nest. We could do this hard thing, live apart for a year, make do. The cabin would be temporary. It was a place to store our accumulated belongings from the big house in North Carolina, just for a year or two—no more than that—until we found the home we felt was waiting for us, tucked back somewhere on a quiet country road. I would be busy with the clinic; she would be consumed by work and classes. The time would pass quickly, we told each other. But I hadn't known then of the days and weeks of fog or the terrible empty weekends there alone.

The tiny cabin was surrounded by dark forest. Trees were stark and bare and their branches bore the marks of bearing up year after year against north winds. Monochrome paled the mountainsides where only weeks before the brilliant colors of autumn had been dazzling. Most of my neighbors on the Knob were seasonal. They left when cold weather came; the crowds of leaf-lookers wouldn't be back up for another year. I rarely saw anyone else as I drove the windswept Parkway to and from work. After a week of cold drizzle and rain, the endless fog gave way to a frigid and angry arctic wind. I stood at the window of the cabin alone on that late fall Saturday morning and felt the wind pulling at the panes, drawing the heat away faster than the wood stove could make it. Over the roof and across the yard brown leaves blew, out over the sad gray bones of the fruit trees huddled inside the garden fence.

That wind was my undoing. It harbored a pernicious misery all its own. You can dress against the cold, but you can't hold out the wind that blows cold to the bone and bears down on the spirit. I was a prisoner trapped inside by the wind and coming to grips with my sentence. These two barren days were merely a foretaste of the winter ahead. The walls of my cell sucked life from me, and by mid-day, the confinement was worse misery than the wind.

Dressed as if I were about to walk on the surface of the moon, I ventured out into a hostile world, and found busy-work making kindling on the lee side of the cabin. There under the back deck, I was sheltered from the abrasive full blast of the wind. Still, the eddies of frigid wind licked over the roof and spilled like a cold liquid into my gloves and down my neck under the old plaid scarf. But the heft of the hand axe and sharp resolve of a clean split gave me purpose. The busier my hands became, the less my mind settled into miseries. I fell into the motions, felt my pulse pick up and my muscles warm.

Then, out of that vast moving sea of cold that spread south from the tundra, one malicious tendril of air licked down and found the scarf. It lifted up the smell of the cedar from our closet back home—what used to be home. The scent filled my memory like a thing alive—the essence of a safe place we had abandoned. The fragrantly brutal truth carried me back to a place I once belonged. Could this have been my life only a few months ago? Peace and security and warmth wafted from those aromatic dark lost places—a memory that made clear the loneliness ahead of us. Under that scarf at my throat a sob swelled, lifted and left on the wind, tumbling down over the garden fence, south, toward Carolina.

༄

I buried the blade of the hand axe into the tough locust of the chopping block and stepped out to the edge of the terrace. The yard sloped away down past the garden into forest and the forest fell away, on and on until forest became a gray emptiness against a featureless sky. I scanned the pale line between cloud and mountain as if I might find an answer there, a clue to explain what was to happen to us now. No answers came. Just then, the wind blew back the hood of my parka and I was no longer under its shadow but under sky. Maybe it was this, at just that instant, that made me look up.

Above me barely higher than the roof of the cabin, an adult male bald eagle floated motionless as if painted on a canvas of low clouds. Each feather was distinct and sharp-edged. His powerful beak parted the wind like the prow of a ship against strong current. Facing into the gale, the massive bird moved neither forward nor back. He turned his head slightly and looked down with one piercing-cold yellow eye, as if he had expected me to look up. Maybe he had been there watching all along, from the moment that the faint waft of cedar had brought me face to face with my new life here. I will never know.

I do know that the overshadowing of those wings was my burning bush. This was my sign, this bird that spread its wings above me like an angel, motionless while the wind lifted him, held him up. This was my messenger come to proclaim that, while there would be strong winds in days ahead that would make us pull inside ourselves unsure of tomorrow, we would stay the course, face the hard times, and make our way forward. The eagle hovered there until the winds slacked and he could move ahead into that force that both opposed and lifted him. Then, the seraph came unpinned from the sky, moved out of the painted canvas of heaven, and moved on. He was heading north.

ℬ

And so here in late October on the anniversary of the day of the eagle, we have climbed to the rim of our valley to look down on what is now our home. Looking back, it seems it has been Providence that has hovered over us as we walked haltingly by faith—from Alabama and Carolina to Goose Creek. At the summit, we stand breathing heavily, facing due south. We remember the day that the eagle looked down on a bewildered man who did not understand then that soon, a few miles north into the wind, he would find home.

Scratch and Sniff

When we get old, it has been said, we do not remember days, we remember moments. Many of my kept moments are memories of smell.

Smell marks moments with memory in ways the other senses cannot. Can you remember from childhood—like new-mown grass, or bread baking—a smell that when it comes to you now, you are transported instantly back? I smell a summer rain and today, forty years later, just a whiff carries me to an afternoon of skating in scuffed shoes on cracked pavement. A hint of Jungle Gardenia and I am at the senior prom. Smell freezes time to a moment in our lives and permanently embeds a memory.

We aren't taught to value what our noses could tell us about the world, and this indifference makes poorer those moments in our lives at which, had we smelled more intentionally for memory's sake, we might remember now more clearly.

I tried to teach biology students the importance of taking in nature with the eyes, and with the heart, but also with the nose. It is my hope that this began for them a habit of "scratch and sniff" that has gone on to enrich their memories of moments in the mountains or at the shore. I like to imagine that they are now passing along to their children this nose-centered way of knowing things, this way of making and keeping memories.

Woodman, Spare That Truck

The kettle on our woodstove hisses around the clock now. The fire from yesterday will survive overnight as coals, and just a few twigs and a handful of kindling will quicken the fire back to life tomorrow morning. If we're not burning wood, we are gathering it. There is a certain comfort in this seasonal ritual, and enough joy in it yet that it still seems new each year.

My experience with wood-gathering has been overwhelmingly pleasant. I love my wood heat. But as I think back over the various chapters in my history as a wood-gatherer, there are a few occasions when the risks and dangers of the enterprise have made me wonder if I couldn't come to love a safe and easy heat pump just as well.

Very soon after moving north to Virginia in March long ago, we learned that we weren't in Alabama any more,

Toto. We were turning blue in our quaint but drafty first home. That winter, we cut wood by permit from the National Forest with an axe and a four-foot bow saw. Our neighbor took pity on our unproductive efforts, and I soon learned by his quiet example to use a chain saw.

I often cut wood with Euell, our kind, soft-spoken, and wise pipe-smoking, country-born neighbor. He warmed our lives forever by teaching me the arts and skills of the woodlot. Even so, there were a couple of times that our wood-cutting camaraderie ended in disaster.

One Saturday, we were cutting firewood not far from town on a friend's land that was to be subdivided for housing tracts. Euell was the master at notching and felling trees. He could drop'em dead on a dime. I was filled with urban admiration at his skill and watched closely to learn from him by osmosis.

There were a couple of other fellas up on this property cutting firewood that morning, away from us, over toward the pasture. Euell and I moved along felling a tree here and there. I watched as he expertly made the notch to drop a tall, thin hickory down between the tops of two larger trees. I stood back as he began to make the felling cut.

Now, theory goes, the tree's trunk is weakened on the side of the notch; then the felling cut drops the tree in the direction of the notch, landing it just where you want it to fall. I had seen him do this perfectly a hundred times before.

Well—the theory goes one way, but this particular tree decided to go quite another. As it began to lean in the expected direction, for reasons known only to the woodland nymphs, it twisted slowly on its base making a little pirouette of ninety degrees. In disbelief, we watched in the direction of the tree's bizarre fall, and what we saw at the last instant before impact was the other guy's pickup truck. His name and the name of his farm were painstakingly wood-burned into the rails that he had built above the bed of the truck. It was these elaborate hand-crafted side-boards that the treetop came down across in a perfect splintering karate chop.

The owner of the truck, some distance away and with his back to all this, was oblivious to what had just happened. Euell was unruffled. He took a slow draw or two on his pipe, not saying anything as we stood there surveying the damage. After a bit, he walked over to the guy and stood behind him, waiting for him to finish the cut he was making on a downed maple. But the man just kept working. Finally, Euell walked up behind him and tapped him on the shoulder. And as the man looked around startled, Euell said quietly and without expression to the wide-eyed stranger:

"I think we kindly busted up your truck."

As he turned to survey the tree that lay across his pet truck, the man's face was that of Sylvester the Cat after Tweety put his tail in a light socket. He was understandably upset by what had happened, but he was civil about it. The good news was that, when Euell told the man that he could repair the damage, it was true. He had the wood, the tools and the know-how to make a fine replacement in short order.

But ever since this experience, I have had a respect for the unpredictable nature of nature, realizing that Mr. Murphy's laws are in full effect, even in the woods.

When a tree is about to fall in the forest, know that if you have planned something so well that nothing can go wrong—it just might.

Good Life, Fertile Soil

When we left Alabama and came to Virginia as young parents on our first great adventure, we lived in an odd rambling house on a large lot in the middle of a small valley town. The shortcomings of our attempts at gardening were clearly visible to the neighbors who could see how little we knew of country living, and they often told us so. I wished I could make mistakes without so much good advice. After six years of looking for land while living in the tiny town, we finally found our place in the country in 1981.

On our little farm homestead just outside Wytheville, we at last knew the blessings of enough space and freedom to live unencumbered. At last we had what they used to call elbow room. There were no overly curious or excessively helpful advisors here in the country to tell me "you can't do it like that." We had the freedom to explore, and to fail in our own peculiar ways, liberating us from the bogeyman of doing things the "way its gen'lly done." We could have a great garden or the freedom to fail miserably at gardening, without critics.

The huge plot I planted in my ignorance and zeal that year was large enough to feed Grant's army; there would be washtubs full of organic leftovers. From the garden remainders, I created our first compost pile.

Compost is one of my favorite memories from that first year of country trial and error. On a cool November morning like this one, I watched the steam rise through the slanting sun; heat waves shimmered above the mound of rotting compost. From an article in our how-to magazines we'd learned to our amazement that you could actually cook a chicken, crock-pot style, in a compost pile if it was tended just right and the bacteria produced enough heat. When I aerated the pile with a piece of rebar, the metal became too hot to hold. I was proud of my compost. But I never did cook a chicken in it. Could have if I'd wanted. There were no nosey neighbors around to report our new Mother Earth eccentricities to the rest of town.

By springtime, that steaming hill of corn shucks and melon rinds, grass clippings and gone-by squash, plus a hundred other bits of green and gold had transformed miraculously into a rich and dark, sweet-smelling humus. The turnings and waterings, snows and winds, and the workings of a million million agents of change had transmogrified dead plants into organic food for the next year's vegetables. Those fruits in turn would somehow fuel the process of building human tissue and powering human thought: the clever chemistry of the countryside.

It has been almost thirty years now since that first garden. We left Virginia, moving back to the big city again and wandered the congested urban wilderness for years before returning recently to the soil in which we grow best. Our children have grown up and moved away, and their parents have become weathered and worn, transmuted by the uncertainty of growing from time to time on rocky soil. They've become something other than they once were.

Different, changed by years, richer in wisdom, perhaps— lessons learned even from the compost: throw nothing away; there is something to be sifted from all of it. Layer upon layer of hope and regret; birth, death; cold tears and warm sun; freeze, thaw; heaps of memory and experience in bits and pieces from the places and people we have been: all of this is altered by the alchemy of time to make a new soil to sink our roots in.

We are mature gardeners now, and our nutrient needs have changed. The medium we are growing in here seems to be about the right mixture of challenge and ease. We have cycled back to living in the country again and for good this time. We have had a wonderful garden this year and I am looking out at a fair-to-middlin' compost pile. And some day yet, I may see if there is enough heat in it to cook a chicken.

Southern Snow

The peppering of ice in countless forms fell from low, heavy clouds last night, drop by grain against our metal roof. Sleet, freezing rain, little balls of snow — I can't say what it was that sizzled like bacon frying in my dreams, crackling on the frozen carapace of our house. I am no Eskimo and I don't have a hundred words for snow. Language fails me when it comes to winter. You see, I grew up southern.

Birmingham, Alabama, in my youth was not a place to know snow. When it happened — only two or three times in my childhood — snow was as magical as any fairy tale I had ever heard or imagined. I remember my first snowfall. When I awoke suddenly, the walls of my bedroom pulsed a strange pink glow and I was almost afraid. I listened for clues to explain the eerie radiance outside and could hear nothing — more nothing than I would normally have heard in our suburban neighborhood. There were no street noises, no distant city noises. It was a deep silence that comes to mind even now when I hear Silent Night. All is bright.

In that first snow of a lifetime, I discovered that some of the things I had imagined about snow were not true, after all. Not all snow compacted into tight, cohesive balls to throw at your little brother or make into forts or for the building of round-bellied men. I might as well have tried to press a cup of dry flour between my mittened hands. I settled for throwing up handfuls of the powdery confectioner's snow, watching it sparkle in the brittle, dry December air. When finally the snow began to clump and stick to my boots, I could hardly wait to build my first snowman.

With a few hints from the grown-ups, I learned to begin with a nucleus of snow and roll it so it would gather more and more snowman skin; roll it until it became so massive and lumpy you and the next door neighbor kids couldn't roll it another time. That would be the base. Roll another irregular ball until it got so big that if it were any bigger, the gang wouldn't be able to lift it up to the second level for the belly part of the abdominal snowman.

As the lumpish snowman parts rolled over and over and began to grow to respectable size, the snow also picked up grass from the yard, leaves and twigs—even acorns. I was appalled. I never saw such dermatological flaws in any of the pictures of a snowman in my picture books— books that planted in my young mind the ideals of true winter. This leprous lump was definitely not Frosty. But there were other winter-snow possibilities! What about sledding?

We called everybody we knew in our Birmingham neighborhood, and of course, nobody that far south owned a sled. But a waxed-cardboard banana box from behind the grocery store broken down flat made a passable run on the neighbor's snow-packed hillside until the box (and our socks and mittens and hats) became saturated with snowmelt, and red-cheeked, we retreated inside for hot chocolate.

We had a big snow the winter I was in the eighth grade. From somewhere, my folks came up with a two-person sled. It bogged down in the slush of grassy places but flew down the icy streets which offered little bite for the runners that were supposed to provide steering. There at the southern end of the Appalachians, Birmingham's south side where I lived was quite hilly. Our house was situated at the top of the mountain. At the bottom of one long, zippy head-first street run on the sled, my brother, who was riding on my back, panicked as we approached the critical turn at the bottom of the hill. In the excitement he hugged my head and wrapped his arms around my face so I couldn't see. We ended up in a storm drain; I still have the scar on my right hand.

Even childhood winter fantasies, when finally birthed into the real world, may not be what you had anticipated, afflicted to one degree or another with warts and a rash. You just hang on to your sled and build your snowman with frozen hands and hope for the best. And you learn, in time, to ignore the acorns on Frosty. Think of them as freckles.

To Us a Child is Born

"The Herdmans were absolutely the worst kids in the history of the world. They lied and stole and smoked cigars and used the Lord's name in vain. They hit little kids and cussed their teachers and set fire to Fred Shoemaker's old broken down tool house."

These are the opening lines of the play "The Best Christmas Pageant Ever." The script sticks in memory because the year our daughter turned twelve, she was the narrator for the community performance and we heard endless recitations. And the following year, we moved to the farm, down the hill from our rural neighborhood's version of the dreaded Herdman kids.

Our place in the Virginia countryside bordered the cemetery of a tiny church. There, on a good Sunday, forty voices sang the shape note hymns. Everyone in the congregation was from five families that had lived in that farming community and had gone to that little brick church for generations. Ann and the kids and I were the rare new members. Warmly welcomed, we quickly became comfortable there.

During summer preaching, the open doors of the church let in the cool breezes. They also let in our black dog Zach who often wandered up the hill and found us in our pew. Just behind the pulpit through the open back door you could see cows grazing nearby against the backdrop of Walker Mountain, twenty miles away through the blue haze. Our kids were loved by a half dozen grammas and they belonged to the entire church. We would discover our youngest sitting with a different family every Sunday.

Across the gravel road from the church, the shell of a one room school house decayed on the crest of the hill. Socks and overalls hung now from clotheslines strung from its corners. Chickens found shade underneath the house during the days, and spent the nights perched in pine trees growing where the school's playground last heard the laughter of children long ago. Rusting appliances framed the front door, testimony of human apathy and neglect.

In the ramshackle school house, a man and woman lived desperate lives, but even so, the county had placed little Mary and Silas there to live with their aunt and uncle. The children were a source of income, but mostly, their support money quenched their Uncle Johnny's thirst for liquor. The brother and sister lived an unruly and impoverished life, deprived of more than groceries or new shoes.

It came time for the annual Children's Christmas Drama. The nice thing, my wife said, would be to ask Mary and Silas to come and take part. Furtive and distrustful, like wild creatures, everybody knew what they would do. Like the unholy Herdman kids, they would come into church and grab fistfuls of cookies and cake. They'd stuff as much as they could get into their mouths and pockets, and then run off. Even though we knew they wouldn't behave and would never participate, it would be the caring thing to ask— especially now, when the other children were so excited and full of anticipation.

It seemed a miracle. They came and they joined in. Mary was even chosen to play the starring role. She sat silently beside the manger, holding the Baby Jesus Doll in her arms, lost in her own thoughts. Silas was a rumpled shepherd who appeared in my bathrobe with the sleeves rolled up three times, a towel wrapped around his head and a broomstick for a staff. He marched solemnly up the center aisle toward the manger, his sister and the baby. In his eyes that night, for the first time, we saw joy and hope.

On that cold December night, two small outcasts were welcomed in. They played parts in a story far greater than the sad script of their own bleak lives; a story of wonder and expectation and the promise of unconditional love.

Of all the little towns of Bethlehem that I've ever seen, that was the best Christmas Pageant Ever.

The Slippery Slope of Winter

There was just me and the cat that year, alone in a cabin on Walnut Knob. Only two of the dozen homes beyond ours on the dead-end road were occupied over winter. The isolation was profound and especially ominous when fog roosted against the Blue Ridge for weeks. And with the fog in winter came the ice. There was one evil ice storm I remember particularly—a day when the White Witch of Winter almost claimed me for good.

It was nearly dark that ice-foggy January afternoon. I groped along the icy road toward home with the truck in four-wheel-drive, creeping along from one fence post to the next as each came into view in the frozen mist. "Stay in the center of the road; don't brake or change direction suddenly. Get as close to the cabin as you can before abandoning ship" I repeated aloud to myself to boost my courage. At least the freezing rain had stopped. Already a good inch of ice coated the wire of the pasture fence beside the road—my only visible guide toward home in the white fog. It was beautiful, but adrenalin is a poor companion to aesthetics, I remember thinking.

Then all the tension melted away like an April snow. The truck lurched sideways across the ice to the edge of my driveway, and came to a stop. I let go my death-grip on the steering wheel and breathed a prolonged sigh of relief, thanking a merciful God for the angels in ice cleats who had managed to keep me out of two miles of frozen ditch. Already I was thinking about the big crock-pot of vegetable soup waiting for me inside the dark, cold little cabin. I could imagine the salty fragrance of it. I could almost feel the soothing heat radiating from the wood-stove and see myself inside, curled up, warm cat in lap, contentedly nodding off during Seinfeld. I was home!

I eased my city shoes onto the glassy driveway, and by holding onto the truck door, was able to stand while I tucked my briefcase under one arm, a sack of groceries from Farmers Foods under the other. I turned to kick the door closed with my foot in the usual fashion, and about here is where the story begins to go, well, downhill.

I had parked at the top of the drive where my intended path would take me a level fifty feet to the porch steps. The other ice-covered lane descended steeply down the east-facing slope a hundred feet to the garden. Alas, the inertia as I kicked the door shut combined with the icy absence of friction sent me sprawling backwards, spread-eagle on the ice, and to my horror, I was trending precariously in the direction of the road less traveled, downhill, toward the garden.

At this cliffhanging moment, I was utterly and completely helpless. I might as well have had my skeleton removed —like Gary Larsen's boneless chickens—so futile were my efforts to rise even to my hands and knees. I lay there motionless. Think brain, think. If I began to slide farther downhill at this point, my body would become a projectile building momentum along the garden path until it came to a jolting stop, jack-knifed around or straddling a tree or fence post.

Each attempt to stand only sent me inches closer to the point of no return. Resistance was futile. In the end, I reasoned that, like the drunk found uninjured asleep in the mangled car who escaped death by virtue of his highly relaxed condition, I must relinquish control and let gravity and fate carry me where they would — a sledding bug on the icy windshield of life.

As I hit the ice, my bags had flown out of my hands. I watched helplessly as my satchel slalomed down past the fruit trees, bounced over the smooth moguls of snow in the yard, swooshed past the garden fence and ski-jumped over the lip of the stone wall, airborne into the dark ice-encased forest and out of sight. I didn't want to go there. Oh Lord, make me a bird, so I can fly far, far, far away.

But I dare not just lay there. It had started to rain again. The longer I was still, the wetter I became. My body heat drained away and the internal gears were grinding slower, weaker every moment. All at once, from want of food, from the delusions that come from a chilling brain and from the sheer absurdity of it all, I began to laugh out loud. Surely soon I would wake up from this preposterous winter dream.

But no. The quakes of laughter were all it took to break what little traction my wet body held against the lubricated ledge, and I began my spinning, spread-eagle slide down the rest of the slippery slope. A sorry tangle of arms and legs came to rest just short of the rock wall ski jump. I was, at least, spared the agony of that particular defeat.

At the edge of the woods beyond the garden where I came to rest, there were trees to clutch. I managed to grab a small ice-coated trunk and pull myself unsteadily to my knees. The silhouette of the cabin roof was by then barely visible against a foreboding, gray-pink sky. I winched my way tree to tree over the ice, back up through the woods and onto the road, exhausted and drenched with sweat even in the frigid cold. At last, I reached the cabin, but my heart sank: the steps had become impassable—an otherwise beautiful eight-tiered waterfall of ice.

My mental and physical resources were exhausted and there was no humor left in me. My first impulse was to shake my fist angrily at the heavens. My second thought was to simply sit right down in the ice at the foot of the steps to see if it was true that freezing to death was actually not so bad once you became numb all over and your metabolism reached the point where thought and pain were merely faint shadows. In my final vision, a brilliant white tunnel of light would point to a place warm and safe, with hot vegetable soup waiting in a golden bowl.

In a last twilight of consciousness before total indifference yielded to defeat, I was able to reach an old shovel under the steps. I busted through the ice to expose enough wood to give a little traction to my soggy Rockports. At the top of the steps, numb fingers fumbled in the dark with the key in the door lock. It occurred to me in my growing stupor that maybe I was even at the wrong house. The world had obviously been under a New Order for the last few hours, possibly under control of the White Witch of Narnia. I wouldn't know for sure until I got inside this door.

The lock turned in slow motion and the cabin door opened. I entered a dark womb of relative warmth, and began to re-inhabit my former limbs digit by digit. About that time, the phone rang. It was Ann, calling from Carolina. She asked casually what I had been up to.

"Oh, I had a little trouble getting home today" I slurred. "Listen: how 'bout if I call you back after I've had a little soup? I can't tell you how badly I need a hot meal." If I had told her, she wouldn't have believed me.

I kindled the fire in the stove and soon it flickered its golden light into the cold shadows. With the cat in my lap, I ate my soup cupped in my hands in my favorite bowl. The last thing I remember is crawling under the covers alone, slipping down, down peacefully into a long dreamless winter sleep.

Hi Yo Silverware!

My idea of removing water drops from the silverware is to take the wire basketful out of the dishwasher and bounce it sharply on the counter a few times before sticking the knives and spoons and other slightly moist utensils into the dark drawer, out of sight and mind. Why bother wiping water drops off flatware that is clean and will sit still and dry without consequence before you need forks and butter knives again? I'm sorry. The horror of water spots is just an emotional trauma that I can't emote. There are some things about which I am obsessive and meticulous, but spoons can be put up slightly damp for my money.

Ann disagrees, and has mostly given up trying to civilize me. We were chatting this morning as I put away the mildly damp silverware—the very same set that we have carried with us now through three states and seven homes through thirty two years of married life.

"Look at this knife. I must have used this one for a tack hammer at some point," I said, as I turned it round in my hand to see the slight dings in the handle. "And check out this fork." I handed her a 40-year old fork that must have come from one of our parents' collections. The tines were slightly splayed, and you could see both a bowing along the long axis and a rotation twisted into the handle as if it had been turned hard while fixed in something solid and unyielding.

"Holli and the ice cream" Ann reminded me. Our daughter had been notoriously hard on silverware, especially when she was in a hurry to get at the rock-hard ice cream straight out of the freezer. Holli always operated by the bigger-hammer approach, and that didn't just apply to ice cream. She was equally hard on the plates, we remember as we note the chips and cracks on what few pieces survive from those days. Ann continued with lore of silverware as I removed cereal bowls from the dishwasher and pretended to wipe them off with a dry towel. She asked me if I remembered fixing a window with a fork.

"Yeah, we had just moved to Greasy Creek. Remember those ratty double-hung windows, the ones we replaced by the second winter there? We were standing in that kitchen putting away dishes, just like we're doing now. The wind was blowing like crazy, like it always did there on that ridge in winter, and the window was rattling so bad we could hardly carry on a conversation. I started to harp (imagine!) about how you had to do something to fix these crummy windows so they wouldn't rattle so."

"You've always had the gift of exhortation" I said smugly.

"Without a word, you reached into the silverware drawer, grabbed a fork, and wedged it between the upper and lower sash of the window. It stopped rattling, alright. And six months later, that fork was still there" she gloated. I guess she thought I'd feel somehow guilty and apologetic over this. It had quite the opposite effect. Made me proud. Show me a problem, I fix it.

Sometimes the solution takes the form of banging the wet silverware on the counter a time or two. A man does what a man's gotta do.

To See the World

Every so often, we are visited by the Old Magazine Fairy. When I saw the plastic bag hanging on our mailbox in the rain yesterday, I knew that the neighbors had left Goose Creek again, off to spend a few weeks in their other home in Richmond. These neighbors pretty much stay to themselves. Neither one of them is well, but they seldom fail to drop off a package for us before heading back upstate. It comes as a frugal reflex for them to pass along rather than throw out, and I'm more than happy to take the National Geographics. And I'm saving every one.

Every time I see the yellow-orange border of this familiar magazine, I have flashbacks to childhood where The Geographic was the closest thing we had to world adventure. Those glossy pages let us explore places we would never go; see in detail and color the bizarre and wonderful plants and animals that inhabit the surreal jungles and rainforest on continents an elementary school mind could not even imagine. We shared the adventures of brave photographers who lived among animals as a way of life, as their job! How could a person stand to simply throw a past-dated copy away, since its contents did not become old when its cover date was past? And so almost everybody I knew back in my childhood had three or four zigzagging columns of National Geographics piled high in the back corner of the guest bedroom: an archive of mystery and the exotic come to Everyman, who was, by those days, already living in predictable and tame suburbia.

৯৯

Down the corridor, a plastic grocery bag hung on the doorknob of the therapy room. Grace had been by. In the bag would be the most recent unopened copy of the National Geographic.

She could see just enough so that, with her red-tipped white cane, she could get to her meals and back in the assisted living apartment building. By feel and by habit every day, rain or shine, she walked alone down the quiet side parking lot along the edge of the woods to the cul-de-sac. When I arrived to begin my work day, I often found her standing there facing the woods that she could not see, staring through her dark glasses intently into the memory of forests.

Grace started teaching biology in high school the year I was born, and even still, she drew peace and joy from nature that she could not see. She could smell the earth change through seasons, feel the wind shift, hear it sigh in tones that told her more than a sighted person could know about the abundance or lack of leaves in the oak forest next to the nursing home. And thankfully, Grace knew her birds by their calls.

Her husband, gone for ten years, had invested in a life-time subscription to the National Geographic. His legacy kept coming, a new yellow cover every month as long as she lived; but since losing her sight, she could not see the images or read the words about the world of sharp edges and color. Her world was becoming each day a smaller and smaller dark smudge of light at the end of a long wooden cane and her greatest adventure, her walk to the edge of the pavement outdoors. That Geographic hanging on my office door was Grace's way of passing on the world of beauty and wonder to those of us who still have time to see.

Kodachrome Recollections

Found. Upstairs in The Very Back Room—a favorite photo of three violets. How well I remember: this was one of my very first flower images taken when I was a newly married graduate student. With my first month's teaching stipend, I bought a camera!

The month was March, the year, 1970. Place: the outskirts of Auburn, Alabama, a short walk from our apartment. Camera: Minolta SRT 101, with a 200 mm lens mounted on the same tripod I have today.

In the photograph, violet blooms and divided leaves are backlit by a trickling brook; light from the water glints and flashes as it flows. By a pleasant accident more than skill, the slow shutter speed I used created a montage of multiple images of petal and leaf against the flickering light of the stream. The photograph has a surreal mood that I have always liked.

But I have forgotten what lay beyond this little brook; I can't recall how or why I came to be there on that early spring day. I don't remember what it felt like to be twenty-four with a new camera or why I wasn't working on my thesis that day. While the camera's vision may be faithful to light and form, there is so much of life it cannot record, and in time, the thousand words each image tells grow cold. What would I have said about and beyond those violets, had I been keeping the words?

It has been a fruitful year of writing the stories that the pictures from Goose Creek cannot tell. What the camera cannot see, the framing in words will gather: the shutter snaps, and one image goes to film, the other to adverbs and adjectives, binding memories in words and pictures.

Butterfly Kisses

As I got out of my truck in front of the house this afternoon, I was regaled by a rising cloud of wispy yellow and black butterfly wings. I fancied that Ann had beat me to the punch and arranged this butterfly welcome. "Wish I'd thought of it first" I said to myself, knowing this was mere fantasy. Later this week, we will celebrate our thirty-third wedding anniversary, and both of us will take extra care to remember it, since on our thirty-second—well, this is how we spent our anniversary last year:

ॐ

I was in the bedroom, fretting over the details of my much-anticipated travels Out West to see my daughter. Ann called out from the kitchen: "Fred! Isn't June 11 somebody's birthday or something?"

I did a cursory scan of the mental calendar and couldn't come up with any birthdays, and went back to figuring out how many pair of socks I would wear in Wyoming. About 5:00 the next day—June 11th—the phone rang. It was my daughter, Holli.

"Congratulations!" she exclaimed. I said thanks, then waited for the punch line. "What did I win?" I asked, in total oblivion.

"It's your anniversary, Daddy. You really didn't remember?"

Fred, the keeper of calendar trivia who can tell you what date we moved into each of the eight homes we have owned, who can quote the date and day of the week he got his first digital camera, and knows for sure the date that we brought the dog home as a puppy—this same walking almanac of minutiae had forgotten his thirty-second wedding anniversary! My daughter was mortified but laughed at the fix I was in. The humor of the situation was lost to me, but not the terror: it was only two hours before Ann would be home from work and my mortal error would be found out.

My first reaction was resignation—to just take my lumps; to do nothing; to throw myself on the mercy of the court. Nathan was totally mortified that I would not only forget but then compound my sins by offering nothing more than an aw-shucks apology. He rallied the troops to action.

Together, he and I created the illusion of forethought. We put a bottle of cheap champagne in the freezer for a half hour, and then hurried it to the most romantic and secret spot on our land. At the head of our valley is a wooded glade where the canyon narrows, the hillsides are lush with rhododendrons and huge tulip poplars. There, the creek pools and plunges down below. It is the most peaceful place on Earth. Ann and I set up a crude bench—an old plank on two big rounds of poplar—and often talked of one day taking a bottle of wine there and watching the sun go down. In two years, that day had never come. We let too many chores and obligations creep into our well-intended slower lives to go there and sit even once.

She arrived home at the end of her workday, tired, but as I expected, ready to take a walk. As we approached the bench in our quiet place in the glade, she noticed the top of the wine bottle peeking up from the ice bucket that was partially hidden under the plank.

"Wow! What's this for?"

And at that instant, I was sure she didn't have a clue what day it was. I breathed a quick sigh of relief. "You forgot our anniversary?" I exclaimed with mock-indignation. I thought briefly about trying to act as if I had remembered all along. But I couldn't live with the deceit, and quickly confessed that I, too, had forgotten the day. Her laughter was very nearly a sob. We had both lost track of time in the flood of daily routine. What pathetic irony in two lives lived so long together and so busy that another year passed since June 11, 1970 is just another day.

I had neglected to bring wine glasses. We passed the bottle between us a few times, thinking back on that June day long ago when we were so young and had such great expectations. Now, here we were, sitting on a plank, chugging cheap wine, so many hopes realized, some regrets, some hope left even yet.

We corked the bottle, packed up, and walked through the pasture arm in arm in the dusk, back to the familiar, the routine, the forgettable everyday mix of joy and disappointment that is the year of marriage.

Not The Way The Story Goes

Setting: Pathetic fallacy sets a pathetic stage. A cruel north-spreading band of tropical storm Bill spills sullen, low clouds and sheets of rain across monochrome fields of blue-green. Ghosts of fence posts and the pale facades of wet cattle fade to vapor just beyond the nearest few.

Characters: You will write about only two. A man, and a dog called Buster. The man and dog are driving to town silent and joyless, along the same roads that just yesterday had made the man smile; smile because each bend offered familiarity and comfort and beauty. Today, he neither speaks, nor thinks, nor feels, but merely reacts to each curve and gust of wind and passing vehicle with its faceless driver. He struggles between the need to keep his psychic shields up against what it is that he must do, and forcing himself to be there, to the end, for his closest companion of four years.

The dog, listless for months, is energized by this unexpected trip. He knows he is going to "puppy camp" since he only travels in the car when he's going to that place of exotic smells and pheromone messages of canine familiarity and comfort, a kind of fellow-feeling he does not get from being with his humans, for all his love of them. For him, this is a good day, even with the terrible, constant pain, eased now only because of something his humans have been feeding him in a little dabs of butter a few times daily for the past week. He doesn't understand all this, but it must be part of the Great Plan that he cannot fully know, only being four years old.

They arrive at their destination, and the dog tumbles awkwardly out of the back of the hatchback. He looks empty and frail, like an old man who has got off at the wrong bus stop, unsettled and confused; and for some reason, he seems to be wearing the rumpled suit of a much larger and stronger man, hollow, diminished, moving away as if in time he might simply disappear. But he is happy to be here now, in the rain, and busily scurries all about the vet office, reacquainting himself with the invisible presence of others of his kind, and he goes through the gate with the nice lady and disappears, forever.

Critical point: The man is a rock, he is an island. He feels nothing as he drives mechanically to an empty house through the tropical storm. And yet, somehow it is easier now, having done this thing that begged to be ignored in the counterfeit hope that one day, miraculously, he would wake up, and this terrible illness would not be so, this duty to his good friend would not be required of him.

But now it is done, the decision has been made, right or wrong. He is relieved, and the lump finally subsides in his throat. He listens to the radio for solace, and sings loudly, as in a graveyard, with some old Motown tune that he never especially liked; but he grasps at it now because it can be sung loud enough to drown out other voices, transporting him to a solace he knows is not real or permanent.

The next song begins and he is pleased to hear the opening bars of a familiar Harry Nilsson tune that he can't quite name. And then the lyrics start:

No, I can't forget this evening
Or your face as you were leaving...
I can't live, if living is without you...

And then like a storm surge, the fog and rain are torn
by the anguished wail inside that car that moves slowly
through a slanting rain; and his pretension ends, his
stone mask crumbles. The song is still playing as he walks
through the mist into an empty house and understands
that loneliness is when there is no wagging tail waiting
for a solitary aging man by himself on a day of driving
gray rain.

Wonders

"Our General...sayled to a certain little Island to the
Southwards of Celebis...thoroughly growen with Wood
of a large and high growth.... Amongst these Trees, night
by night, through the whole Land, did shew themselves
an infinite swarme of fierie Wormes flying in the Ayre,
whose bodies being no bigger than common English Fly-
es, make such a shew and light, as if every Twigge or Tree
had beene a burning Candle." Sir Francis Drake 1577

Ann and I and the kids sat on the front porch steps of our
first place in the country, six miles from the small Virginia
valley town of Wytheville. This was our first night in the
new house—a house that did not seem to be ours yet,
would not for some months. It was not our front porch
or our pasture or our road yet, but we began that night
to allow that place to belong to us as we would belong to
it. The same warm, barely perceptible evening breezes,

insect noises and indefinable aromas fill our view from this front porch on Goose Creek in July more than twenty years later, so the moment is easy to recall.

The horizon some miles away appeared as a faint gray-pink outline each time the thunderhead flashed lightning over Grayson County to the south. There was no thunder, only a whirring chorus of bush crickets, katydids, and a hundred voices that were new to us. Fireflies began to emerge from the tall grass, first a few nearby, then by the hundreds, twinkling candle-lights that floated above the meadow and up across the road by the old abandoned house and weedy field. To the vanishing point they rose and blinked and signaled. Cool flickers of amber and lime, punctuating the indigo darkness—some lights sustained, some staccato code, many rising during their brief pulse, others falling. The females waited patiently for motherhood on the tips of timothy grass.

Then, the headlights of an approaching car beamed over the pasture ridge, sweeping briefly across the meadow as the car turned away. And I imagined that, with that signal, hundreds of the thousand fireflies blinked in unison in answer to this greater light. Yes, it happened, too, at times when lightning was near enough to produce stroboscopic shadows of trees along the road. Yes, it was true: at times a small cadre of these lowly luminous beetles worked together briefly in the same language, synchronized by light—a language they both produce, and understand.

But consider this greater wonder: in a few places in Thailand and Malaysia, every single firefly in an assembly of thousands blinks no more than 13 milliseconds before or after its myriad neighbors, producing a stunning strobo-scopic chorus of light alternating with brief periods where every last one of the thousands of them all pause together for a short while before starting the giant synaptic pulse once more. Compounding this oddity, it happens closer to home—in the heart of the Smoky Mountains—where one can see synchronous fireflies. There it begins in one part of the cove, and passes like a human stadium wave to include every part of the super-organism that can encompass many acres of woods and field.

There are languages spoken all around us—in flashing lights and midnight stridulations, in whiffs of animal aroma, in the very silence—that we do not have the senses to perceive. Even so, I sit on our front steps in the dark on a summer night, quiet as a field mouse, and listen.

Part Four:
Rooted, Grounded, Found

Alpha Male Bonding

It is common knowledge that Labradors love the water. These retrievers were bred to swim out into the waves and fetch fishing nets in the frigid waters of the North Atlantic (and were originally called Newfoundland Dogs). They have heavy insulating coats to keep them warm when wet, and even have webbing between their toes that makes them excellent swimmers.

Tsuga, our yellow lab pup, joined the family two months after Buster left us. On his second day here, I couldn't wait to carry him down to the edge of the water knowing what joy it was going to be for him to discover that he would grow up a free-ranging dog on a place with two creeks right out his back door. What a lucky dog!

My excitement on his behalf was dashed when I discovered that he was not only not interested in the water, but was actually afraid of it! Maybe the fact that there was motion and noise set off his alarms; his nose offered no signals of friend or foe from this long undulating creature. In his short lifetime in this strange world, all the water he had ever known was mirror-still in a round plastic bowl.

But a week later and on his own terms, Tsuga was ready to get his feet wet. With a purpose, he hopped off the end of the foot bridge by the house this morning and headed straight to the shallow current of the branch. It was as if this was something he had finally mustered the courage to do, and must do quickly before his fear could talk him out of it. Into the trickle he jumped with all four paws and attacked the muddy bottom, sending up a spray of black muck. In a matter of a minute, for the first time but certainly not the last, he became a mostly chocolate yellow lab. The pride of accomplishment beamed from his muddy face, a face like a child making mud pies, proud to be really dirty—like a grown-up working dog. Now he needed a bath in the creek for sure, but I would let him decide if he wanted to face the bigger waters today.

I sat at the edge of Goose Creek near the barn while young Tsuga explored in the high rushes and grasses by the stream. He came cautiously to the brink and put his paws just barely in the current with comical ambivalence, pushed ahead by curiosity and genetics, held back by a native fear of the unknown. What was this motion and flash of water all about? And why did he feel so drawn to it now, as if he had been there before? In the end, his drive to explore won out; he pounced with all four webbed feet into two inches of cold, flowing water. To my surprise, he flopped down on his pink tummy in the stream for a few brief seconds. And in two shakes of a puppy dog tail, out of the water he tore at a rip, heading for the safety of the house.

He stopped. You could almost see it happening. "Wait a minute. I'm wet, a little cooler, but I'm okay! I'm safe! And that was fun!" So he circled back to me, and lay there on the cool gravel, in the shade of the crook of my legs. The cosmic consciousness of all Labradors had found him, heart racing, chin down on his paws. Then, creeping on his belly, he approached the water's edge, and in he plunged once more, running around wildly in the widest part of the stream. Again and again with growing confidence he tested the waters, and each time, he returned to me for sanctuary.

It was the funniest, dearest-doggiest thing I had seen since Buster left us less so recently, and I laughed until I cried. This is not a figure of speech. I cried: for the beauty of that moment, for the pure goodness of the sunshine; for crows and ravens and goldfinches all around on a clear, crisp autumn day. The tears were for the innocence of a young life that I was allowing to fill the place of one I still remembered and missed so much. Tears were for the rightness and goodness of this new bonding with another intelligent spirit and for the transience of it all. There is a goodness in these rare moments that is beyond words and overwhelming. Thank you, little buddy, I needed that.

Falling

There is a certain exciting melancholy in the coming of the first fall-like days—a letting go and a welcome all together. I sit here in the cool shade with my feet stretched out into the slanting sun's warmth and comfort and watch yellow leaves of walnut and locust flutter and sift toward the spent soil of summer. Tiger swallowtails lift and spiral as if to put those yellows back in place for just a few more days.

The forest is still green from a distance, but a closer inspection will show you that no leaf is untouched by changes that shorter days have brought. Their surfaces are lightly filigreed by insects that could not have made a meal of them in the healthy prime of summer. Striped maples show patches of discolored spots, red and yellow circles like ringworm, where fungal threads wind their way through the spongy spaces between upper and lower surface of the leaf.

Soon the fungi and bacteria will consume blade and petiole. Like a thrift store shirt, its matter will pass on and on, handed down until there is nothing left but buttons and a few bare threads.

The Truth Plain and Simple

I've been asked more than once what we plan to do with this land. Knowing the answer they expect from the owner of six fallow and fertile acres along a creek, I could tell my neighbors that someday we will fence it off to pasture a few head of cattle; or that we might plant Christmas trees like so many other landowners in the county who can't make their land pay for itself by farming alone. But I believe that from now on, when they ask me, I will tell them the truth: I plan to use this bottomland for taking spider web pictures.

That should make for some raised eyebrows, don't you think?

Savoring Autumn

It is a mercy that leaves in their dying do not suffer the same putrescent decay as animal bodies. There is so little to a leaf—it is mostly air and pigment. And when a leaf's job is done, there remains only the empty carbon shell of summer industry. They steep into pleasant aromas like tea leaves in the last warmth of late autumn. In a grave-yard of leaves, Death is nostalgically fragrant.

Listen. Can you hear in the gentle susurrations before first light the papery sounds of leaves jostling, still clinging, barely, to twigs where already the watery sap is heading south for winter? Summer leaves are supple and soft, and do not rustle and clatter like fall leaves after rigor mortis has set in. But the death rattle of fall leaves bears little grief since already, the young buds of spring's translu-cent greens are forming in that place where a death has overtaken the stem.

Look. Underpaintings of ochre and sienna and titanium yellow show through as the chlorophyll blush passes from each leaf in dying like a watercolor wash. Watch as a walnut leaflet falls twirling about its axis, falling in a straight line without fanfare. The maple leaf, unbalanced by its heavy petiole, rocks stem to stern and twirls in a dizzying circle along a spiral path, not giving up gracefully before joining fallen fellows on the lane by the mailbox. I sometimes have to stifle applause after a particularly brilliant performance.

It is early yet, with so much more to come. I should keep a list of autumn's pleasant details to look back on from the short days of February. Yesterday while gathering wood over behind the barn, Ann stopped as if she had heard something off in the distance or was trying to recall some thing forgotten, staring unfocused as people do when remembering. "Peach cobbler that ran over in the stove" she said. And she was right. And so here is yet one more potpourri fragrance of fall, an unknown but familiar sign of autumn we can add to our list. There will surely be more.

The Thrill of the Hunt

Hunting season has arrived. My neighbors hunt while I stay inside and read and tend the woodstove for the several weeks of deer season. Already, the camouflaged boys in pick-up trucks are cruising slowly down our gravel road planning their strategies against things in the woods. Soon, Ann and I will be wearing our blaze-orange accessories every time we go out to get the mail. We should probably dress the dog likewise.

When I was a boy, I knew that one day I must become a hunter. It was the way a boy became a man. I fished. Why shouldn't I hunt? Finally when I was twelve, I got my first air rifle. This was no small victory since my mother's father had been killed by a gun in a hunting accident long before I was born. Wasting no time, in my back yard I took my BB gun and shot a dove from far away. Hitting it was trivial in the way cartoon dynamite or dropped anvils are, without much effect. No real injury done, a few feathers fluttered down and the dove flew away.

A few days later, I aimed at a small yellow bird sitting on a telephone line. This time, there was no cartoon comic relief. A large bloody spot marked where the bird's eye used to be, red against yellow and black feathers, and he fell to the ground at my feet. This was the first time I'd seen a songbird up this close; beauty and blood left a lasting lesson on a young boy. There were more serious consequences to hunting than I had known, and I understood then that I could take a life, but I could not give it back.

Life feeds on life. We could not live in this place if the death of other creatures did not sustain us. But maybe I do not need to hunt for the reasons that my neighbors would give. It is true that many a family in Floyd County lives off venison to supplement their diet and to make the month's income go farther. But to my way of thinking, many hunters may be drawn with such enthusiasm to the woods and fields this time of year because hunting gives them a purpose to be out in nature, a thing that grown men, and especially city men, find difficult to justify without such a manly intent as hunting.

Is it possible that the thrill of hunting is something in the stillness and chill of the dawn air? Maybe a hunter feels there in the woods like he feels nowhere else—part of the whole of things, vital, integral to the economy of nature, alert and watching. Every nerve cell, every one of the senses is attuned to the slightest changes of shadow and light, to the smell of rich earth, to the faint rasp of a beetle under bark, and the sound that leaves make when they fall to the ground. There to kill, the hunter may never feel more alive, and think, perhaps, that it is the killing that brings the exhilaration.

Still and quiet under lavender clouds at sunrise, I sit in our woods up the valley and feel the same rush of adrenaline, senses sharp, not separate from tree and earth and sky. I sometimes go there with the pretense of hunting with my camera, but mostly I know it is not even about bringing back images, other than in memory. The pleasure is merely in being there, and this alone can be my purpose and my quarry.

Changing of the Guard

Just when we humans are starting to wind down our daylight busy-ness and go inside for the night, thinking how good it's going to feel on these cooler nights to pull the covers up to our chins, there are other creatures that make good use of the nocturnal side of the human day—lives lived while we dream.

First as shadows lengthen late in the day come the birds that feed overhead. Chimney swifts and nighthawks sweep the air with wide open mouths, scooping up invisible insects that rise like a cloud in the billowing thermals. Later will come the mammals that harvest the same in-flight feeding niche—the bats that we see mostly as shadows against the sky, black against deep indigo, erratically finding beetles and midges and moths by sonar. And last night, just before we reached the barn coming home from our walk at quarter 'til dark, a screech owl trilled from the edge of the woods. Deer snorted and huffed indignantly as if to tell us we were infringing on their shifts, that we should go indoors, and give them their due share of solitude and sky.

With the shorter days, the nights are beginning to chill and there will soon be no insects at dusk, and those that feed on them will move on to find other work to the south. The deer will hide from hunters back in the steepest woods; and the owls will own the crepuscular day until spring comes.

Slow Living

Ann and I have settled happily and for good in Floyd County. We love it here; it feels right for us. But apparently, this slow lifestyle is not for everyone.

It hasn't been long since I found myself defending our decision to live the way we do. An acquaintance, newly transplanted to Blacksburg from a large Mid-Atlantic city, lamented her new "life in the sticks," as she called it. This seemed odd to me since she was living in a large apartment complex in the bustling middle of a large university town. I felt obliged to educate her about the real rural living we are accustomed to.

I described our pleasantly isolated setting where there is only one traffic light in the entire county, and this, fifteen miles from home. I told her about the twisting gravel road that we live on, at the far corner of this quiet county.

"Where do you go to get STUFF?" she asked. "I bet it takes you forever even to get to the pavement. How do you stand it? Give me a traffic jam any day!" I swear she actually said this.

"You can only go slow on our road, and that is why we like it. And traffic is never jammed in Floyd County" I told her, with both satisfaction and pity.

At that instant, she labeled me as a cull from the fast, urban society of her experience and preference. I couldn't stand the heat of modern life, she surmised, and so I had fled the kitchen and "gone rural." Gads! What if she was right? For days I was oppressed by a mood of self-doubt. Why had we abandoned the swift main current of society and opted for a life in the slow lane? What did this say about the time-values on which we had built our new family rhythms? Over the next week these questions ruminated in a deep place, submerged below the surface of conscious thought.

In our preferred country lives we are as active as anyone anywhere, I told myself. We can't be faulted for running away from things to do. But there is a difference between being busy and being hurried. Our slow gravel road protects us from hurry. The shady lane becomes a kind of watchful meditation to prepare us for entering the faster world in a slower state of mind.

We approach each blind curve with care, and on slowing down, see the graceful way that light slips past hemlock branches and how the eddies of the creek flash in the shadows of rhododendrons. We would never see this on a fast road. As we near home one bend at a time, our meandering road becomes a welcomed part of the detoxification ritual that brings down our blood pressure, calms our racing minds, and brings us to center again on the simple act of living here in the present moment. I imagine I am as busy as my city friend, but I know I am not as hurried.

Minding the Winter Wood

The body has a kind of memory unknown to the mind, its cues and prompts coming from the feel of things held by hands, joints flexed just so, tension held here, not there, a certain line of sight more than the thing seen. I cannot stand behind someone at the computer and tell them what steps to take to complete a complex task, even if it is something I do mindlessly a dozen times a day. It is only after I sit down in the seat, put my body in place, and feel my way through its steps that the sequence for the task comes flowing out my fingers to the proper keys in perfect order that only my hands understood. I find it is the same way with building a fire.

It has been almost thirty years since the first time I fumbled with strike-anywhere matches and crumpled newspaper, and gathered the three stages of kindling that build a quick fire. The routine unfolds unconsciously when my body moves into that certain configuration, kneeling before a cold stove. Each motion is stored in the moving parts of torso, eyes and hands, in the timing and sequence and plans that the soma uses while the psyche attends to other matters on a cool early morning in October. Suddenly a fire pops and sizzles in the stove behind me as I type, and I am barely aware that my hands contributed to its presence.

And yet, considering as a whole the home industry of wood burning, I cannot imagine a more intentional and premeditative endeavor than heating a house with wood. My calendar runs two winters ahead to cut, stack and cover wood to dry for the long winters to come. In January, my week is governed by the snowstorm that is expected as the weekend approaches. Will I have enough of the right mix of high-heat maple and oak and smaller quick burning starter wood under cover from the snow? My morning fire anticipates the day ahead, and I load it full, or put just enough in to keep some coals, acting as the house's thinking thermostat and weatherman all together.

I know the source of it from the forest, and can often say precisely where any particular piece of stove wood fell to earth. After four winters here, I know the temperament of this old house, and I understand the moods of the stove itself. I have a sense of how it will draw in all manner of winds, of when it will need ashes cleaned and how long with the present feeding it will keep the kettle hissing happily on its cast iron top. Heating with wood is both a discipline and a reflex; it requires constant attention to comforts in the present but always with a distant gaze ahead to provide for months and years of cold that will surely come.

Traces

After it first falls, thick and smooth, deep enough to cover gravel and ground and all traces of autumn, I go out hesitantly into the new snow and leave the first blemishes in the unbroken white. In the beginning, there are just the boot tracks to the woodpile and the signs of the dog's quick trips out and back. For a time during the storm, these trampings will fill with the sediments of the next wave of snow, leaving smooth undulations in the surface. But life goes on, and one can do only so much admiring from the windows. By yesterday, there were tracks—our own and others—that showed what a busy place our seemingly-deserted valley really is in winter.

Over there is where the dog and I went down to wade across the creek, to rummage through the barn for the snow shovel that we needed for the first time this season. And there, past the garden, I'd remembered too late to retrieve my maul, and you can see where I rooted around with the toe of my boot to find it buried under six inches of snow next to a rounded mound of split cherry I could smell even through the snow. And those human tracks going back into the valley are not mine; they belong to the friend who called this morning and asked if he could hunt our land. He left a while ago, carrying out only his deer rifle.

Turkey tracks loop back and forth in the pasture between Nameless Creek and the opposite ridge along the old pasture road. Grasses that stick up from the snow have been nipped along the turkey trots. Here and there, the snow has been scratched away and the frozen earth bothered by prehistoric scaled feet, grubbing up a meal. At times their three-toed tracks suddenly disappear half way up the steep bank, and I know they took wing, ponderously, and only because the bank was too slick with snow for their heavy bodies to climb. Maybe they were startled to flight as the dog and I took our first walk along the creek this morning. They will roost in the tall pines up top of the ridge and be back making more tracks down here tomorrow.

Deer tracks are everywhere in the morning, each hoof mark a sharp pair of converging crescents in the shape of praying hands; they are creatures of the night. In the daytime, against the snow, their gray-brown disguise is laughable. Only when they run up the hill away from us does the white flag of their tail match their winter hiding place. It is in the snow during hunting season that they are most vulnerable. And about that, I have mixed feelings.

I cannot think of a greater contrast than deer blood in snow. Another hunter—a neighbor whose family has lived in this valley and along its rim for generations— came a few late afternoons ago and took down a buck that was so familiar to us we felt like we knew him, though he never had a name. This eight-pointer showed up often and very near the house, standing majestically on the hill above our back porch. He looked down on us, snorting indignantly as if we were the intruders here.

Now his blood spotted the snow, just beyond the garden by the split cherry wood. The hunter will bring us some of the venison. And I will eat it, and be thankful for that gentle grass eater so that his death will not be in vain. I am a reluctant vicarious predator and carnivore living in a fallen world.

Since the kill, when the wind is from the west, as it often is, the dog stands just out the back door with his nose in the air, pulling from the aromasphere traces of an unfamiliar yet powerful species memory. This young dog has never killed, but it is still in his wild nature—covered, barely, by a veneer of domestication and breeding—to hunt and to chase, to clutch a pulsing throat with powerful jaws and meat-rending teeth and to taste blood. The taste of blood of any creature—chickens, sheep, a newborn calf, a deer—will sometimes cause a dog to revert to the inner wolf that hibernates there, the killer that lives just beyond the veneer of our domesticated world.

We're expecting rain later today. I hope it will rain a lot. Tsuga and I will stay indoors while the rain washes away the red snow and the tracks and all the traces of wildness, past the garden, across the road, and down into the cold creek.

Asleep at the Wheel

We're morning persons. For us, after 8:00 at night is getting late. At that magic hour we begin the sluggish, groggy gravitation toward bed. While there are gradations all along the continuum toward full surrender perhaps by

9:00, the transition can at times be alarmingly abrupt—a most striking translation in a matter of moments from full waking frenzy straight into a sound sleep.

A few nights ago, I finally slowed Ann down enough to have her listen while I read a revised essay about an eagle, written a few months back. It runs a bit more than two thousand words and we would need maybe eight to ten minutes to read it through. So, Ann and I curled up on the couch next to the wood stove. She leaned back against me while I read aloud to her.

After the first page of my apparently soporific reading I could feel her body twitching, starting at the feet and working its way up. "The twitches" are well known in our marriage after decades of sleeping (or reading aloud) in proximity; the twitches indicate the brain has relinquished control of the muscles and joints and is about to give itself up to Technicolor dreams. I nudged her. "I heard it all" she startled defensively before I said a word. She had heard, perhaps, the first page, and then gone abruptly off duty. Oh well. I needed to hear it read aloud myself.

Then, last night, in a rare flare of late night fervor, she decided she must have access to the computer to type a letter well after 8:30. Sure, she could displace me in the midst of my half-hearted writing; I'd go over to the couch and hold the book in front of my face and feign reading while she typed. Slumped back on a soft couch next to the warm and comfortable wood stove after the witching hour of eight is hardly the best reading environment. After five minutes of eyelid watching, I looked up to see how Ann was getting along with her project. There she sat a bit off-center in the chair, but I could see that she was typing feverishly. And yet, from across the room, the Word document on the screen had an odd sameness. I got up and went over the desk to investigate.

She had typed one and a half paragraphs of a message to her sister followed by ten—now going on eleven—pages of the letter "k". She had fallen asleep at the wheel, and was careening down the road between the guard rails with her foot on the gas, oblivious. I woke her gently. She mumbled something incoherent and trudged sluggishly through the bog of narcoleptic quicksand toward the bedroom.

"Seems to me your should replace all the k's with the letter z" I told her, chuckling at my cleverness as she fell into bed. She appreciated my humor that night no more than she had been impressed with my oral reading the night before.

One day, we'll both nod off at the same early hour, while a skillet of bacon sizzles on the stove and the tub of water overflows onto the bathroom floor and into the hall. After clearing the greasy smoke, the rescue squad will find us in a sound sleep—one on the couch, the other in the office chair at the computer. They will call our children who will find a nice home for us so that we do ourselves and others no harm. And that will be fine, as long as we can expect lights out at the home no later than seven o'clock. We wouldn't be much good in a Bingo game after that late hour anyhow.

Succession

When we rounded the corner to see this place for the first time almost five years ago, we discovered that its eighty acres was bisected by a state road. I immediately lost interest and drove on past. Our vision had always been to have a piece of land (twenty acres would have been gracious plenty) with a long, private lane to the house nestled in the very heart of the land; we would have the ideal buffer from road noise and other intrusions—our private, quiet hide-away. But there it was: a road that ran smack between the house and the old barn. That a road divided the land was only part of my initial disappointment. The steep north face of the valley had been ravaged by loggers—from the looks of it, less than ten years earlier—and lay stripped and tattered. It broke my heart.

Ultimately, though, my aesthetic objections were mollified by the joy of discovering the charms of the old farmhouse, the wonder of the two clear creeks, and the narrow end of the valley along Nameless Creek that had largely escaped the loggers. Maybe we could make a home here after all, I decided. And here we have lived now just a bit more than four years, in the house on the winding and narrow gravel road with grass growing up between its two tracks. In all this time, I've spent very few hours on the cut-over north slope back of the house where today, we went to select our feral Christmas tree.

The aerial photo of the place from the 1930's shows that all of that steep land behind us was in pasture then. On the few occasions we've pulled ourselves up that near-vertical property line, sure enough, we've found the old split chestnut rails that once kept cattle from wandering off into tall woods. At some point in the forties or fifties, by design or neglect, forest took over the pasture by the natural process known as "old field succession"—the predictable, gradual and orderly changes that will replace one set of forest transients with permanent residents over time.

By the early nineties, mature white pines dominated the abandoned south-facing field in this process of change. The trees were large enough to sell to indiscriminate loggers who came in 1994 and took everything they wanted, ruining three or more hardwoods for every massive white pine extracted. They cut roads deep into subsoil; in places, it remains bare of vegetation to this day. After the ravages of the logging, to maximize for regrowth in pines that were planted after the operation, the hillsides were sprayed with herbicide. There is no going back to undo what has been done. We can't change the past, but we can change the future of this forested hillside and will try to be better stewards than the last folks who saw the forest only as a source of profit in the short run.

In the summer, the thirty five acres behind the house has been our berry patch. The open canopy lets in a flood of sunlight. A thick tangle of blackberry and raspberry canes has filled in the hillside beneath skeletal standing pine trunks left from the logging. In July the vines cascade heavy with fruit, blue and red, spilling down over the trail like the hanging gardens of Nebuchadnezzar.

When we first hiked up to the top of the north ridge that first year, there was an impressive view of the valley, the house and barn, and the two creeks far below. From two hundred feet above our roof, any place you stood on that south-facing ridgeline you could turn a full circle and see nothing but sky and ridge and treetops, and the green wedge of our valley through the standing pine trunks. Ridges beyond ours go on and on, and it's easy to imagine you're in the midst of an Appalachian wilderness. I pretend that the devastation on our hillside was caused by a fire—a lightning strike—a dozen years ago. It makes the ugliness seem less personal to think it exists in its present sad state because of an "act of God" and not from the carelessness management of man.

The planted pines now are almost ten years old and a dozen feet tall. In places they grow together thick as a hedge. Soon a new forest will obscure the wider views we once had from behind the house, even from the open berry-picking paths that follow the old logging roads. Time will come that it will be impossible to walk up there at all. Every pine with its whorls of five or six low branches will soon touch its neighbor's branches like interlocking arms, turning back would-be walkers. Ten years from now, the blackberry and dewberry and raspberry vines will grow spindly and fruitless in the new shade. The place won't be much good then for bringing down twisted and yellowed Charlie Brown Christmas tree culls like the one we cut today.

The abused and tattered land behind the house is not a great place to go for a casual stroll. It is not a place for beautiful pictures. But it seemed to me today, being there, that it is not somewhere I should avoid because of what it lacks. I should climb up there often—now, while the joints and muscles still work; while there are memories to harvest in the form of berries to pick and pathetic un-loved pine trees to bring inside for a few more Christ-mases. But mostly, I will go up to find a quiet place facing south toward the low winter sun, to sit and be still among the standing bare pine trunks and fallen hardwoods and the briars and the old chestnut fence rails.

It is amazing, really, all that has happened here. This was a pasture where cattle grazed. Before that, virgin hemlock and oak and white pines tall as ship's masts grew in dark forests seldom visited. I wish I could have seen it then. I wish I could see it fifty years from now when it will have begun to seem like healthy forest once again. But I only have today—a fixed point in the succession from past to future; and I'll try to do a better job of living in the land and in the time I have here.

Frozen In Time: Moments in Winter

The glassy snow and treacherous ice of a week ago is slushy enough to walk on safely this morning, even with a fresh overnight coating of frozen fog and freezing rain. The hemlocks along the creek, ravaged by a foreign hoard of indifferent and ravenous insects, are slowly dy-ing. Their branches hold more frozen jewel drops of ice than green-gray needles, a sad kind of beauty.

The deer have come out of storm seclusion. Lying low during those days when it would do them little good to browse for grasses buried under crusty snow, they are saving their layer of fat for more productive foraging. This morning, their pronged prints come right up to the front steps and show signs of a brief stop to munch what is left of the Hostas by the footbridge.

Swollen with snowmelt, the creek runs both under and on top of the thick ice-quilt that mutes and modulates the more familiar sounds of a summer creek; water has learned a hundred new permutations, variations in the key of winter. Listen. The visceral core of creek runs hidden except in round patches of open water, dark against white. Green waters part around a rounded boulder here and there and the world is full of flow, smooth and quiet as an Arctic island.

Out our window, juncos leap for tiny seeds of broom sedge, their cold feet leaving cuneiform slits and wedges in the snow, like crop circles out of nowhere. There is play in their work, tiny swingers of birches. Their antics in a motionless world are reason enough to have hope for spring.

Field Notes: December Creek

Cold currents stagger
Down the stairway of a mountain stream
Drunken and grumbling,
Muffled like empty kegs rolling
Over an endless flow of steps
While a distant crowd cheers

※

Marvel: that along a wooded stream, the eye can adjust without a blink to light intensities from mouth-of-the-cave darkness in the thick shade of rhododendrons to the blinding brilliance of unfiltered sun, amplified by ten thousand lenses of frenzied water.

※

The smooth rocks are slippery with a thin gloss of edible film, a living layer on which snails and larval stoneflies feed, and trout upon them, and so on up to the chief predator, which would be me. It is a heady experience being at the top of the food chain. And perhaps an illusion. Regimes, too, have to eat.

※

Consider the creatures that live their lives in the calm cleft of the torrent, under the edge of a rock, sheltered from forces that would sweep them away. This is where I want to live and I think of home as such a place.

❧

You kill a smooth stone by taking it out of water, its clarity and luster, sheen and hue drying a pale death before your eyes.

❧

Reflexively I pulled an itchy speck from the back of my neck. Between my thumb and fingers an organic excrescence a moment before had been a living green half-inch worm. You just never know when your time is up.

❧

A leaf falls into moving water, one final trip that enacts its monogram, the letter "L". It begins the stroke more or less vertically, with a flourish of flutters and spins in air. It hits the water with a tiny gasp. Whisked along straightway by the current in the horizontal stroke, it is held up safely by surface tension for tense moments with hope it might survive the trip to the open sea. It takes on water, listing as it flows, a few smokestacks above water yet. Finally foundering in an eddy, it is lost with all hands.

❧

Transience: I accept that all these boulders, fixed and hard, are far from their birthplace, passing through. They are every bit as moveable now as the day a thousand years ago when they were dropped here, borne along effortlessly for miles—as easily as a child's rubber duck that spins and lurches along the spring branch. Boulders are not fixed. Nor am I. We both bear the illusions of immortality, my failing body and these falsely immutable stones.

꽃

A water strider is only the suggestion of a creature,
A wisp of wire and thread
That walks by faith, its changeling shadow
Of globular gray paddles fringed in sharp mirrors
It moves against current, just enough

꽃

When I was a child, a grown-up told me that sounds
never die. Their waves spread out in space like ripples
on a pond as big as the universe. Then somewhere, the
sounds from my childhood in disordered dilution still
live. I wonder if it is into moving waters that lost sounds
go. I am sure I hear them in this stream but cannot understand, only that they are happy released from its surface.

The Manual Transmission of Winter

We've always driven stick shift cars. There is an intimacy
in the bond that develops between the driver, the road,
and the machine that is missing with automatic gears
that act as if they know the road better than the driver.
Our road climbs, the engine pulls, and the driver makes
the necessary adjustments to find the gear that suits con-
ditions as they change from moment to moment, mile
to mile. And so it is with our lives here in the country.
A time of changing gears has happened. We hear the
changes, sense the new rhythm in the engines of our
lives, in the smells and winds and in the way the air
feels around us.

Wardrobes shift as the season grinds into low gear. Now when we go out, it is not a spontaneous walk, come as you are, out the door and into the woods. Not only must we give care to make the transition from house garb to outdoor garb, but for almost every item, we'll don not one but two of everything: two shirts, two pair of pants, two pair of sox. We will make every outside excursion count now, stay outside as long as we can, and dream up things to do with our gloved hands before we have to come in and take it all off again.

Starting today, the woodstove will hold a fire round the clock, every day, until the January thaw. It is the home heating equivalent of chain smoking: one fire does not go out but helps light the next one and the next. The fire will burn constantly from the winter thaw until the first duplicitous freakish warm days of early March that we will know are only cruel, taunting lies. The last embers will go cold, finally, only after the killing frost of May that we thought would not come, and so planted tomatoes the week before. It's all part of the rhythm, the manual transmission of life here that has become, now in our fifth winter, so familiar. We anticipate shifting seasonal gears, knowing that snow-covered roads lie ahead, not happy for all of them, but ready.

Field Notes ~ First Snow

The woods are dark and snow appears illumined as it falls, following the verticals of bare poplars on the hillside, flakes falling in perfect perpendicular to the flattened grasses of the pasture, each flake or cluster of quills along its own path and not another as if lowered down, down one by one on invisible threads. Most distant feathers float suspended and, picking out a single one to follow with the eye, it will take an eternity to sizzle to the ground on its immense journey. One from half the distance falls twice as fast, and tufts of flakes just in front of my face zip past in a terrible hurry.

ॐ

Snow falls onto the creases of my parka and does not melt. What had looked through the windows like falling flakes are not flakes but aggregations—light loose thatches of tiny ice needles, linear and sharp-tipped—loose feathers of filamentous crystal down. There is no sign of a six-sided lacey flake in any of it. The locks fall from the shoulders of my jacket onto my arms, white against the dark of my coat like my hair shorn from the barber's shears, slivers of gray and white, they tumble softly to the ground.

ॐ

The true white of snow recalibrates my perception of colors that I think I see when snow is not there for comparison. Against the snow, the white house, newly painted two years ago, already shows a graying in the paint and a dun dusting from the road that seems drastic against true white. How odd the yellow dog looks against it. His markings become conspicuous—especially the darker places on his back legs above the feet, the tip of his tail and ears—all show red-foxy tones. When he stands on the hillside, his darkest parts match the leather-brown broom sedge that stands bent in the snow.

❧

From the front porch, even over the burble of the creek, falling snow hums just below the threshold of human ears, hisses as it falls like tiny droplets against a hot griddle far off. As snow falls, sounds are muted and flat just as the details of visual texture are now absent from the forest floor, making me snow blind and snow deaf—a partial dampening of sight and sound that is both comforting and unsettling.

❧

With only a slight suspension of disbelief, walking across the pasture full of snow I can imagine that I am moving barefoot along a vast shore of the finest white sand. It blows across the road, a soft cold powder; there is not much difference between a drift of snow and a dune of sand. Dry snow squeaks underfoot like Daytona Beach on spring break, and you dare not go out onto either without sunglasses. In the high stepping, labored trudge through our field, I might as well be walking back through loose sand to the hotel along the boardwalk on Myrtle Beach. Even though the smell of everything is all wrong, one calling seagull overhead would just about complete the illusion, but I'll not wait for it to come along today in this cold wind.

❧

The pasture grass, cut once late in the summer, lies matted down almost completely by wet snow. Thin tips of orchard grass bristle up here and there from the white field; it wears an unshaven and haggard look. The turkey hunt out these grassy whiskers as they stagger across the field in their loopy forays for food.

Yesterday, snow fell in soft lines against the dark hillside. I set up the tripod on the front porch because that is where I could go in the snow without changing out of my slippers. The hemlocks on the ridge are dying. That this makes me sick with sadness is one of my odd sensitivities, I suppose. Yet here is one in view that still has needles enough to hold snow. See the regular, graceful way they spread their dark arms just so? And snow falls flake by flake, in such depth of distance, so matter-of-factly, each a creation of its own predictable unpredictability of form and beauty.

Solomon's Sheets

As days grow colder and the ominous gray of winter descends on our little creek valley, we look forward with dread once more to the battle of the thermostats. Hers is from Venus, mine is from Mars. The wife and I may never find the Goldilocks "just right" happy medium when it comes to winter comfort zones. Except in bed. And even this has not always been an island of peaceful thermoregulation.

In our otherwise perfect marriage, there has always been the irreconcilable matter of the sheets. In the summer, cotton is no problem. Cool sheets in summer are pleasant to both of us. And I am—but she is not—perfectly happy in winter with these same cotton sheets. I know that when I crawl between layers of chilled cotton in January there will be that catatonic instant when the body will go rigid and breath will come in short, shivering gasps. In my Martian opinion, this bracing chill is merely an anticipatory appetizer to the ultimate warmth that will come—eventually. I argue with the wife that this shock is painfully pleasant, not unlike the transition from an ice-water plunge to the blissful relaxation that will follow in the warm sauna. She says I must be from another planet.

The wife between cold sheets is pitiful to witness. On cotton sheets in winter, she turns an instant blue, stuttering and convulsing; and as soon as the lights go out, she becomes a shape-shifting heat-seeking parasite whose boney appendages conform to every nook and cranny of my agitated unsleeping form. If she's cold, we can forget the demilitarized zone in mid-bed. In the pursuit of nocturnal warmth, she will slink and slither well across that line, leaving me pinned on the very brink of my twenty percent of the bed, sweating from uninvited physical contact.

After a dozen or more years of uneasy winter bickering, at last she discovered her nirvana: flannel sheets. On that first night of flannel, she slipped between soft power-blue fabric and commenced to making embarrassingly contented sounds. She was so happy with our new linens that I tried to love flannel too. But after a week I decided I'd rather spend eight dark hours naked in an electric wool sock than to sleep under flannel. She pulled 'em up, I threw 'em off. She purred contentedly, I fanned the covers all night, with nightmares of slow death by Crock Pot.

It looked as if we were doomed to live divided in two-thermostat household. Many a marriage has ended over controversies more trivial than this. The Solution came to me one day from King Solomon's voice that boomed from heaven. It said "Divide the baby." And this was the inspiration for our Marriage-Maintenance Hybrid Bedsheets.

From the dilemma of being either too hot or too cold, we have resolved the controversy in a way that is "just right" for each of us. We severed one cotton and one flannel sheet down the exact middle and sewed the halves together to create a full sheet that is half electric wool sock on her side of the bed and half Polar Bear chilled cotton on mine!

While this may not be the Final Answer to World Harmony, it is my small contribution to the war between the thermostats. So. Rest in peace, guys. For my next project, I'll be working on a solution to that eternal conundrum of extraterrestrial cohabitation: does the toilet seat stay up or down?

Renaissance

Birds were calling outside my window this morning in the dark long before I was aware of their sounds. We hear what we expect to hear, and for so long through the winter, there has been only the wind, the creek, the hum of the computer, the yawning dog stretching in his sleep in the next room, the ticking of the woodstove and no birds.

When bird voices finally broke through winter's oblivion just now, I could not name them. That kind of familiarity with the particulars of life outdoors will return soon enough as I comprehend I am no longer alone in a gray-numb world of winter.

First light lured me with my coffee out onto the front porch. A comfortable flannel shirt was just enough. Beneath the raucous sound of the creek, spring was humming underground. I could feel it through my slippers, through the soles of my feet.

March wind carried a trace of sweet loam, moved faint red buds gently at the first hint of dawn. March is to June as early morning is to noon: there is not much color yet in the day, or the year. But the sun will rise. And it will come sooner tomorrow and stay later, every day adding more tint to the faint dilutions of February.

By late April, the color will be almost more than an eye can stand, and I will sit down on the front steps all hours of the day enveloped in a full pallette of artist's colors. The east sky is pinking up already.

The pasture grass is smooth as a putting green painted butterscotch, pressed down flat as pancake batter, snow after snow. Five black crows move erratically back and forth across the field like ice skaters, leaning forward, arms tight against their sides, gliding in the twin choreography of hunger and curiosity.

NeitherNor

The grass out the back door piles up in unkempt tangles, dark green, growing explosively from winter's unspent reserves; and this morning it is dusted with a skiff of late March snowflakes. The birds—titmice, bluebirds, robins—sing from bare branches, come down to the cold ground hungry and wonder, why did they arrive South before dinner was served?

The only color, save for hidden greens in the pasture under last year's dead dun and taupe, is the yellow-greens of the tiny flowers of spicebush along the creeks and edge of the field. Every other color this time of year is high overhead in the red buds of maple and sarvice and cherry that are brilliant when the sun shines brightly. But that is just the matter. Just when all of the rainbow potential of nature is being birthed so fast you could hear it if you truly listened, the season of NeitherNor descends with a vengeance in late March throwing a cold, wet blanket on the party.

It has been three days since we have seen the sun. It will be another week before we see it and warmer temperatures again. We will endure another week of tiny fires in the wood stove because it is just cold enough for the house to lose a few degrees too much heat at night for the next day's comfort. We will endure another week of wet mud before the garden can dry enough for tilling. There will be one more week of sepia-toned somber days that are more like winter than spring.

Then. The sun will suddenly appear with all its bags as if it has come to stay. NeitherNor will be a memory of a time when we needed a bit more patience than we had for life to return to our lengthening days. And it will be for all the world like a surprise party where out pops the world of color again. SURPRISE! And the yellows of bellworts and field cress, the maroons and reds of trilliums and columbine, and the whites of bloodroot, hepatica and anemone will explode all at once, as if they had been planning this event for months. And then it will be spring.

Not Our Fathers' Forest

Last week we enjoyed the gift of a beautiful early March Sunday afternoon—a sampler of what spring will eventually be like when the new month finishes pitching its tantrums and bipolar mood swings. Ann and I were inside, resting between bouts of outdoor cleanup under the warm afternoon sun, and the dog had been escorted to his alfresco lodging to dry off from his last romp in the creek.

A short while later, while reading the Sunday paper, I looked up to follow the dog's "somebody's here" bark to its apparent source over in the pasture. Sure enough, two dark figures ambled unhurriedly from the head of the valley—bold forms against the barley-colored field of winter-flat grass. We rarely see walkers, so I waved hello from the porch as they approached Goose Creek and ambled the hundred yards to the barn, to greet them and chat a while.

My neighbor introduced her friend Emily, who it turns out, was no stranger to this valley or the old house that has become our home. It's always very grounding when people we meet tell us "oh, you live in Marvin's place", or substitute any of a half-dozen other names of farmers or hippies who have been connected to "our" house. They still hold claim to it in memory, though Marvin and Larry and the Boones are moved away to other parts of the county, or another state; and one rests behind our house forever as ashes under the maple tree, we are told. Ann and I are just passing through and neighbors who have lived here longer than we have are good for putting belonging and roots in perspective.

"I see you tried to grow fruit trees" our neighbor said, pointing toward the strips of aluminum foil still spangled from the dead form of what was almost a yellow delicious apple tree. The deer had eaten all the leaves off it two years ago in spite of all our mint-soap, dog urine, pie-pan attempts to protect it.

"There's a cold pocket down here along the creek, even if the deer would give us a break" I told them. "We're thinking maybe some cold-hardy pear trees might make it if we can build a high enough fence." And the conversation shifted to other kinds of trees.

"You know, the woods are not like they were when your home place was built here. We built a deck from locust we cut off our place just twenty years ago, and already it's going to rot."

Black (or yellow) locust is widely known for its resistance to rot. "A locust post goes into the ground the day you're born, that fence post'll still be standing when they put you in the ground seventy years later" I had heard when we first moved to Virginia thirty years ago. How odd that the properties of a species could change like that, we agreed. We speculated maybe it had something to do with the locust leaf miners that plague these trees every summer. Maybe those little beetles that lay eggs in the leaves keep the trees from putting down as much fiber or something, we supposed.

Emily, who was quite knowledgeable about fruit trees and forests and gardens, also offered as how these hills used to be filled with all sorts of big cherry trees, many producing a bounty of free fruit that you just don't find anymore hereabouts. I agreed that, both here and over on the edge of the Blue Ridge where we used to live, there are the standing remnants of massive cherry trees— gaunt, heavy-branching ghosts—yet another species that seems to be going through some kind of change in its role in the forest. Curious, we said. Insects? Weather? Who can say?

It was the very next day that I happened to read an article about the damaging effects of ozone on forest species— particularly vegetation in mountainous areas where the impact of ozone (and acid rain) are more severe. Some plant species have ways to protect themselves effectively from high ozone levels; others do not. Blackberry leaves turn red in summer from ozone damage—an indicator I'll watch for a couple of months from now. And, according to this study, black cherry, whose absence we were lamenting, shows a 26% growth loss from ozone and other pollutants down in Shining Rock Wilderness in Carolina.

And the locust trees? Maybe it's not just our imagination that you can't count on them to make lifetime fence posts like the old-timers used to. It is not the same wood because it's not the same forest that grew here when we were born fifty years ago. And fifty years from now, neighbors may meet under the walnut by the barn and exchange pleasantries on a warm March day, remembering those who have lived here in the long-past. There was that fella who wrote all about this place way back. Remember? And isn't it a shame what's happening to the oak trees all around?

Clothes That Make the Man

The fire in the woodstove this morning was kindled from habit and not necessity. Last night was far warmer than we've been used to through winter and we—or at least I—could have been comfortable today without the fire. It isn't here yet, but the gears are shifting to a new season. We will move from wool to cotton, from long sleeves to short, and spend more of our day outdoors in the longer light of spring. We will happily molt that layer we've been obliged to live in for every trip outdoors. But then again, there is a sort of melancholy in laying aside the rituals and fabrics of winter dress.

When the first days of autumn come and cool toward winter, I am secretly excited to dig out from storage the flannel shirt, then the sweatshirt and jacket, and finally the heaviest coats and gloves I own as the cold descends and the snows come. It was this cold-weather costume change I anticipated, even as a young man in perpetually balmy Alabama. For one born with the mountains in his blood, it was this challenge of bundling up against the best shot that Old Man Winter could hurl against us that made me dream of places to the north, wrapped against the imagined cold in my blue Eddie Bauer parka on a warm Birmingham night.

Less bulky fibers and styles have come along since 1974 that keep me just as warm but don't give me the lumpy, segmented look of the older-fashioned down garments. I don't wear that parka now, but I still have it, keep it nearby and will never give it up. It hangs in the entry hallway, its final home, a constant reminder of where we've been and hoped we were going. I couldn't bear to part with that coat, although one time I did, reluctantly and only for a couple of months in the spring of 2001.

After his junior year in college, Nathan decided that he was meant to experience more profound north-ness than his parents. He found an attic bungalow in Bar Harbor, Maine, for the winter. We thought he planned to hike the coast of Nova Scotia in the spring, but instead he informed us, to our dismay, that he meant to walk home to Goose Creek on the back roads of the Northeast. There were still good people, he told us, who would surely take him in along the way. (And thankfully, he was right.)

I mailed him my parka before he started south in April because his anxious mother insisted, since it was still the warmest and most compressible, backpack-worthy winter wear I owned. I relented grudgingly, my possessiveness almost entirely wrapped up in the symbolic significance of this one old coat. It had been a portent of our need for winter clothes and the new life we imagined to the north that required them. It had foretold the rhythm and pace, the march of the seasons, the changing of the gears in the manual transmission of winter that is so familiar to us now—like the feel of a worn, soft garment against our skin.

Of Pink Bunnies and Blue Jars

It was the best of times. All morning she'd been working on our granddaughter Abby's Bunny Cake to take down to Carolina the coming weekend. "Come look!" she called proudly from the kitchen. I had smelled the sickeningly sweet confection baking since well before first light.

There it sat in all its pinkness—a round-faced caricature, sized such that it would just barely fit in the traveling cake carrier. It was a something with long ears, but for the life of me, it didn't look like a rabbit. Wrong nose. Wrong mouth. And I opened mine. Big mistake.

Some while later, after a period of intense silence from the kitchen, agonized wails woke the dog and startled me from my meditation from somewhere within Photoshop.

"It's ruined. I've worked so hard on this and I knew I shouldn't have put whiskers on a rabbit! Why did you make me do this!? I can't start all over! It's hideous! Little Abby will be terrified!" And thereafter the words melted into undecipherable sobs of failure and blame.

Earlier, I had suggested quite casually that, if she wanted whiskers, maybe toothpicks tinted with food coloring might work, and if not, she could just pick them off the icing. She chose not to follow my advice and used lines of chocolate syrup instead. Moments later, it bled into the pink icing (of course) and smudged all the more when she tried to fix it. By the time I returned to the source of the wailing and teeth-gnashing, it was a rabbitoid creature most hideous. I suppose I did not make matters any better when I made light of the dark smear of a short moustache as I goose-stepped out of the kitchen gleefully singing "Here comes Adolph Cottontail... " I should know by now that my zany efforts to make the best of unfortunate culinary disasters are not appreciated at times of grave domestic crisis such as this.

It was the worst of times. But when the fog of feminine histrionics had lifted an hour later and the cake icing had dried, all signs of Adolph were blotted out by fresh pink icing, and all was well with the world. The day might be redeemable after all.

And I mention this story of the depths of wifely angst only to contrast it to its opposite extreme of emotions toward the end of the very same day—a study in the mysteries of the filters and lenses that gender's hormones and synapses impose on our disparate world views.

This Day of the Cake was the first pleasant spring day of the season that our perky and vivacious local pharmacist was not at work. By mid-afternoon, she was up to her hip-waders in mud where her happiest moments are spent digging in the boggy banks of the branch that runs beside the house. Ostensibly, this grubbing is to clear the flow of rocks and clumps of grass that have fallen into the foot-wide rivulet—a responsibility in the name of beautification and matters of flowage only a "branch manager" like herself can understand. But the deeper reason she loves playing in the little stream is that the wife is a wannabe archeologist.

From the banks of the branch, she has unearthed two rubber ducks from decades past; old fence insulators; scraps of red-rubber tire inner tubes, vintage WWII. Found are shards of crockery and broken canning jars—lots of broken canning jars.

But with today's discovery, our intrepid explorer of mud could not have been more excited had she unearthed the Lost Ark of the Covenant. Out of the silt poked a glistening edge of pale blue-green glass. Down on her knees in the wet grass, she teased it out slowly from the sucking muck that had hidden it these past—who knows?—fifty years. Giddily, she carried it down to the creek and bathed it inside and out, carefully as if it were a rare Etruscan urn. Then it came inside to the archeology lab for soap and mild abrasion to bring it to full luster. By dusk, it was time to call Associated Press and have them send the photographers.

It gleamed there on the kitchen counter in the late afternoon sun, its blue-crystal letters standing in relief from the abraded but intact surface: ATLAS ~ STRONG SHOULDERS ~ MASON it proclaimed. Buried and full of the sediment of the ages, it came to light on a day that started in defeat; it ended in the thrill of this small victory.

If I'd had any idea such an ordinary thing would make our archeologist this happy, I would have collected a case of masons from antique barns and old country stores and held them in reserve in a secret place. I would have pulled them out one by one on those doghouse days when disaster struck in the kitchen—those wonderfully horrible days when all I could see in the calamity were macabre mustachioed rabbits and an amusing story for my journal.

The Spring that Couldn't Quite

It is almost the middle of April. According to the calendar, we've had just about a full month of springtime. But this morning there is a fire ticking in the wood stove. Our heavy winter jackets hang behind it, drying from the cold soaking they took on our rain-or-shine afternoon sanity walk around the middle loop yesterday. It seems all too familiar. Last year, spring was so wet and cold that our bean seeds rotted in the cold ground and we couldn't re-plant until late June—late enough for the bean beetles to peak just when the crop was setting fruit. Tomato plants sat there, inert, like plastic mock-ups. The corn, as high as an elephant's eye the summer before, was not as high as the dog's before we turned it under, earless in August.

Bloodroot and Hepatica are up, here and there, but their petals stay clutched tightly against the cold wind. Trillium leaves poke up along the edge of the creek, but they are no taller from one day to the next and I half expect them to change their minds and begin shrinking back under the leaf litter where it is less harsh and gray than above ground where wet people walk their walks.

And actually, I hope it stays drizzly and overcast today. I am holding two mental images from yesterday's walk that I want to capture with the camera, and those pictures will vanish if the sun shines. They are the kind of snapshots the brain is better at than the camera—beautiful in their subtlety of lighting and color but too busy in composition. The life goes out of the image when a tiny detail is taken from the larger context, and the visual is too little of the being there with all the senses.

The first vision: crystal water drops hanging in the mist from tiny lemon-yellow tufts of spicebush flowers; and second, the translucent paleness of last year's birch leaves that hang on until the new leaves push them away later in this anemic spring. I'll try to bring these beauties down off the ridge as images in my camera, but I make no promises these will satisfy. Sometimes, you just have to be there.

We need the rains we're having this week, and if the weatherpersons are right, we will see sun and upper sixties by the weekend. Warm weather will come, but it may go again. It is taking its own sweet time deciding. Meanwhile, we'll just be happy we still have a little dry firewood left and plenty of hot chocolate and a warm puppy beside us while we browse the seed catalogs, traveling hopefully towards summer.

Color My World

It is the translucency of spring that I look forward to from the middle of winter. It is this, more than the season's growth or warmth or change in the view that I anticipate. In mid-April, sunlight will travel ninety-three million miles to our woods, to shine through a thousand thousand tiny see-through leaves. Packets and waves of light enter chloroplasts in that space within the diaphanous thinness of an emerging leaf.

Spring leaves take in sun but they do not hold onto it. Like a ghost through a wall, spring sun shines into and through. An April leaf projects a chartreuse glow on the world that you will not see when leaves have grown to their full size and thickness in summer.

Keep your "whiskers on kittens". A new leaf in spring is one of my favorite things.

Mystery Perfume

We walked the dog around the pasture loop this morning and noticed that one of the grass species had flowered overnight. Its tall spiked inflorescences punctuated the field all around us like exclamation marks above the lesser grasses, white fleabanes, black-eyed Susans and yellow clovers. Each grass inflorescence is spangled with countless tiny anthers that release a cloud of pollen at the slightest touch or breeze. Could this be the source of the mystery smell?

I'd already told Ann as we walked out the door that I was determined this year to find the source of that elusive smell that we've encountered the past three summers since moving here. It is everywhere and nowhere present and in quality, sickening sweet, but oddly pleasant. We don't know what it is, but when it comes to the valley again for the first time each June, it is familiar and comfortable as an old friend, nostalgic as only remembered smells can be.

My theory has been that it comes from a wind-pollinated grass rather than an insect-pollinated flower (except possibly a high-blooming tree flower—basswood has been on the suspect list). When I shook the pollen from the spiky grass today and inhaled it, there was no trace of the mystery perfume. This isn't where the smell is coming from. I'll have to keep on sniffing.

Later in the day while picking wild black raspberries, we found a common milkweed with some flowers that were just beginning to open. Its mauve five-clawed flowers certainly give off a very sweet, almost too-sweet smell, but this plant is not abundant enough in our valley to create the inescapable sweetness we walk through in early summer. What else could it be?

There is also a strong bit of this smell in the bark of the maples when the sap rises and oozes from sapsucker borings to blacken the bark with dilute "syrup" in the spring. But I have to put my nose right on the bark to bring out any of that smell. So this can't be the source of the mystery aroma either. And I've been struck before by the smell of wild honey while walking the woods in years past when honeybees were still common. This everywhere honey smell is like our unknown, but ours has a Bit-o-Honey overtone, if you can imagine, and is more cloying than honey—oily, almost oppressive in its omnipresence.

In time, I'll put my nose to some grass or weed, pollen or petals and have that moment of Eureka! discovery that will solve this fragrant puzzle. Curious. In a way, I'll be sad the day when I finally know. That day, there will one less mystery and one more fact in my life. These days we have a surfeit of knowledge, and knowing too often becomes the end of a thing. But wonder and curiosity send us out—looking up, turning rocks, scratching and sniffing, inhaling deeply—awed, receptive and ready for surprise.

Just As He Pictured It

Imagination is a peculiar place of the mind: a balmy desert island; a glowing cavern deep in the earth where dragons live; a jungle populated with talking animals. These places exist in childhood when our imaginations form much more of our understanding of how things could be than our limited young experience informs us of how things, in fact, really are. Life is either much better or much worse in imagined places than the place where we live. Imagined places that are worse than where we live make us happy for our own warm beds and even for our scolding mothers who are much more to be desired than the green-faced warty witches who live beyond the dark forest in that other land. Better places—even if in a land far, far away—allow us to tolerate the annoying younger brother and the bully who lives at the end of the block, because someday, we'll be kings or knights or super-heroes; we'll find chests brimming with rubies and doubloons in a land of eternal sunshine and perpetual dessert, or discover an old wardrobe with a secret back door. Maybe then, we'll live in those imagined places, happily ever after.

Once upon a time, the boy became a man, grew up, and moved away. He learned what science said the world was really like. Soon, he had started a family and then lived in many houses in many different places when one day, he began a new job in an empty office. They told him about the warehouse where cast-off things were stored and that he should go there to see if a desk or chair or goose-neck lamp might be useful for his bare quarters.

Among other ordinary things, he found a picture on the dull water-stained wall, off in a far, dark corner of the dingy old warehouse. It was unlike any other picture the man had ever seen. In it were trees and sky and wa-ter—ordinary things, to be sure—but the man swore that he could see himself in the picture. He could enter the picture and look all around him—up at the sky, down into the water, at the plants in the forest that he knew by name and saw in the imaginary world of the picture. He remembered as a boy, in the land of his imagination he had known a place just like this one. The creek was full of fish and under every log, a brightly colored salamander lived. Brilliant birds sang in the trees. And it was always different, each time he went there. The light shimmered in the leaves overhead—first the leaves of spring, then of late summer. At one moment it was sunny and fair, the next cloudy, threatening, smelling of rain.

And he knew he must have this imaginary place, inside its frame, above his desk in his new office.

It remained there on his wall for him to see, every day, good days and bad—days he was happy to be where he was and days he longed to find his place, out and far away from the jangled congestion and unpleasantness of noise and clutter, away from cities, highways and shopping malls. He hoped someday to find this place of the imagination where he spent so much time each day on the banks of the silver creek, under golden trees with the ever-changing sky overhead.

In time, he moved to a new place. "Maybe this is the last time" he told his wife hopefully. And they settled for a while into a small cabin in a beautiful country place. But it was not yet home to him. While he enjoyed his walks along the peaceful lane down to the edge of the mountain where he could see forever, there was not a trace of his beautiful creek with the silver sky he had known from the picture that now hung on the wall of their modest cabin. They had almost given up hope of finding the home they longed for. And just when they gave up struggling to find it, it found them.

At first, it was not a place the man even wanted to stop and inspect. The old house looked as if it might fall in from neglect. The land had been beautiful at one time, but the most uncaring of loggers had left behind little of that beauty. "No, No!" insisted the wife. "This is the place." She brought the man back many times over the next few days to learn what it was that called to her there. One day they walked on the land through briars and tangles along a grassy road that had seen few, if any, travelers in many years. It followed the slender valley further and further back where the valley grew narrow. At last, they rounded a bend where the forest had grown tall and escaped the logger's axe. The trees arched over the creek. The creek full of bright fish glistened as if it were made of polished silver. Shadows dappled the dark earth under the grand old trees. And all at once, he knew.

"This is the place in the picture. This is the forest and creek I have dreamed of since I was a small boy. This is the country place I longed for all these years while the picture hung on my office wall, both taunting me and giving me hope that there was indeed just such a place."

They moved to the valley and in the old farmhouse, they live to this day. The picture is there, too, across from the hearth, above the old piano where its travels have come to a pleasant end.

The man wondered the day he first saw the creek of his dreams, and wonders still—had he not held this image in his mind and in his heart so tightly and with such hope all these years, would such a place as this have become real at all? Would this peaceful valley along the silver creeks have even existed for him to find? Was this place created by the power of imagination and longing? This is a thing that he almost believes, and something that he will never know for sure.

Ecology of Ownership

Eighteen trees! I touched them one by one as I counted them thirty years ago in our very first back yard. I swelled with the pride of land ownership. This lot in a small Virginia town held our own personal forest we would enjoy as the leaves changed through the seasons out our back door. Or if Ann and I decided that we needed them for firewood, we could cut them down. Like the house and the land they grew on, the very trees now belonged to us. Ownership seemed to confer absolute dominion over both the land and everything on it.

When we moved to our second home, a little farm a few miles outside Wytheville, that first forest of eighteen trees was dwarfed by our wooded hillsides that covered twelve acres. We tended that land, pasture and forest, and grew to care about it greatly. We owned it, but realized, too, that it nurtured and sustained us and we owed it our best efforts to use it wisely. What would happen to it in the hands of the next owners? They could do with it whatever suited their values and their own particular land ethic. It made us sad to know that our influence on this familiar green triangle of land would end the moment we signed over the deed.

And now we are making our home for good on Goose Creek. We walk the trails that our feet have worn beside the creeks and along the ridges. Soon now, once again, there will be blackberries to pick behind the house from the timbered clearings where a young white pine forest grows with adolescent vigor. From the top of these hills in every season we see beyond us the grandeur of the natural world. But without protection after we're gone, it could all become nothing more than a commodity—a realtor's gem to be clear-cut, then dissected into smaller and smaller tracts over the years.

This month after living here in Floyd County for four years, we may tie together the last loose ends of a conservation easement. This agreement will confer some legal encouragement on future owners to keep this valley a healthy whole as they use it wisely and enjoy it as we have. And there's a larger hope to our efforts. By itself, this property here is just a small parcel. But combined with the land of adjoining neighbors who may also put their places under conservation easement, together we can preserve whole intact watersheds and unbroken stretches of forest ecosystem on the headwaters of the Roanoke River. The health of both the natural and the human community here and in our region will the better for this.

Today we walk under a canopy of a thousand trees within our boundaries. But we'll always recall those eighteen in our first tiny back yard that made us consider our relationship to and interaction with nature. Since that initial flush of ownership long ago, we have become convinced that, since we are only here for a while, we are really just caretakers of land and trees, stewards of creeks and ridges. We don't own these bones and organs of nature any more than we own the air we breathe or these bodies that we use for our short time here.

These young poplar, hickory and basswood trees that we brushed past on our walk today will grow tall, and someone—perhaps our great grandchildren's children—will play in their shade or pick berries under them decades from now. They, in turn, will become the caretakers of this pleasant grove and in that possibility, I find considerable solace and hope.

Dog Days

This morning I discovered that the white lawn chairs were missing from the back porch. Curious. I found them later, over behind the barn, positioned facing the southern sky, down the valley away from the house, just right for a great view of the Dog Star and its August companions.

My son and his friend had been out in those chairs last night, under God's heaven, in conversation until the wee hours—not inside, watching a video, playing computer games, or off in a bar somewhere.

Finding those chairs out in the pasture is to me a hopeful sign that maybe our kids are unusual, in good ways that matter, because they grew up in the country and because our entertainment has come from the things we were able to find in our back yards and pastures, and the sky above us, right where we live.

Aural Vignette

"Come" I said, motioning for Ann in the kitchen to follow. The two of us stood on the front porch in the darkness, listening.

Morning on Goose Creek in the September of our lives sounds like this: drops falling from dew-wet branches; bush crickets whirring, one from a goldenrod along the pasture whose song blends with the next, higher up in the meadow, and a dozen more in monotone requiem to summer past; and beneath all other sounds, and around them, the rift of water over rock, falling into the hollow of itself, a spattering, tinkling liquid philharmonic of peace.

If there were no humans on earth, this is what the world would sound like. And there are two, standing utterly still, and thankful.

So This is How it Ends

This is not like me. Usually as fall approaches, I'm revving up to full throttle in anticipation of the cool, invigorating months that are the best time to be alive in the southern mountains. I'm not sure what's wrong. Maybe it is the anxiety of knowing we don't have enough firewood yet to see us through until March. Or it might be the near-certain approach of yet another in a series of potentially devastating late summer hurricanes. Ivan will be here by Thursday with his mindless power and fury. The rain will fall on the godly and the ungodly alike, on the prepared and on the indifferent. The waiting is hard. But the chief cause for my discomfort, I believe, is the regret of having to say goodbye to the summer garden never quite full born.

There is sadness in the warm air at the end of a summer remarkable for its coolness and constant rains. We get little enough sunlight in this crease of valley in the best of summers. Sunrise brightens the garden in July around nine in the morning and it is in shade by four. But this summer's garden has been a dreary embarrassment. The soil never warmed, and the sunflowers mocked the fact that there was no sun. I called it my Gothic Garden. Instead of looking at it admiringly at every opportunity, like a doting parent puffed with pride, I found myself avoiding eye contact. And so today's goodbye was good riddance. Apology and regret; hope for better fortune next year.

I cleared away the failed beans, the listless vines of half-formed squash and the legion of rampant galinsoga and chickweed. The weeds, more than intended vegetables, represented our summer crop. They grew luxuriantly in the half light and mist, in the neglected gaps between weak spurts of gardening zeal. Cleaning off the garden today was to finally sweep this year's failure off to the compost pile—out of public view, and mine.

Today for the last time in 2004, I cranked the tiller. Its dull tines turned the weedy residue into the clammy earth still wet with Atlantic Ocean moisture from last week's hurricane. When the work was done, I walked behind the lethargic machine at a plod—step; pause, step. The engine hummed in monotone pulses. I pondered how it might have been in the days when a garden failure like this meant a lean, hungry winter to come. I was a farmer reluctantly putting his old mare up to barn for winter, knowing he'd failed to feed his family, with the heavy yoke of disappointment and dread weighing on his drooping shoulders.

Plod, plod. The thick treads wobbled over the planks I'd thrown down between the banks of the creek. Then one last climb, my mechanical mule crept up the ramp and onto the barn floor. The red machine had stayed out in the garden all summer this time, covered with a tarp, a permanent fixture for four months, waiting for a dry spell. The bright metal gave the only color where nature's greens and golds should have grown. Now that the tiller is under roof again, the garden is officially closed for business.

I am unsatisfied, incomplete, and restless. It is a time of change beyond my control. In less than two months, one of the major candidates is going to be in the White House. It feels like a national kind of autumn. I won't be gratified, whatever the outcome in November, and am deeply sad for our country and the difficult seasons it faces.

I need the physical work today, a new purpose for the season, now that the failed garden is gone by. I'll deal with this blue funk by felling at least one of the standing-dead ash trees at the head of the valley, back where Nameless Creek and the pasture road converge. Grappling with the heft of firewood will yield a product, something I can show for my toil. I'll have a couple of truckloads of white wood to stack close at hand, just out the back door where I can look at it and see, finally, some fruit for my labor.

And yet, it is a fragile and yielding discomfort that I suffer. Let me see the first migrating Monarch while I'm bringing in the winter wood, and God will be in his place, and all will be well with the world again. And next year, we'll have a great garden. You'll see.

Home Economics

The standing corn browns and curls and our deep valley grows colder in the shadows of the shortening September days of '05. The canning is laid by, and we celebrate the end of long months of kneeling servitude to the trowel and the watering can. We look forward at last to reclaiming our days from the tyranny of the garden. But our glimpse of freedom is a false and short-lived interlude of recovery; our responsible guardianship only changes in the fall from gardening to the unending care and feeding of the woodstove.

We decided many years ago to heat the house with wood as long as we are able. Every fall I have to explain this logic to myself one more time, just as I find myself standing in garden mud in the humid heat of early August when I blow the gnats out of my eyes, questioning the economy of being a grower of vegetables. It would be so much easier just to pay and be a consumer. But we garden; then we gather wood—two self-inflicted but mostly joyous burdens in our year, not all that different in their end products or purpose, or in their impact on our lives for good.

Neither heating with wood nor growing a year's worth of garden vegetables is the path of least resistance, greatest convenience or efficiency of our finite personal energies. In both these labor-intensive endeavors, there is the illusion of control over our lives in at least these small ways. I feel very much like the omnipotent dictator as I plan my attack on woodlot or corn rows. But when I am honest with myself, I have to acknowledge my utter dependence on the workings of sun-heat, rain-sap, and soil-plus-time.

I carry the heavy, dirty pieces of wood one by one from forest to the truck to woodpile to stove; I stoop, bend, tug, water, hoe, weed, lift, and harvest each of a dozen varieties of prolific root and fruit. And in the end, I must confess that in all this, I am just the midwife standing by with relatively little control and little to do with the process but collect what nature makes of her own secret raw materials.

Our comfort over winter that comes from filled canning jars and wood's warmth depends on the internal wisdom of roots, trunks and leaves. It relies, too, on the integrity of our woodcutter's tools and gardening utensils and the strength of these bodies of ours. All must work, together—nature, tool and human hands. Our woodpile and the yellow, green and gold canning jars lined up like functional art in the dark vault of the cellar are testimony that—for one more year—we have lived in a blessed harmony with our wits, our own bones and with the land that somehow sustains us. The full warmth we will feel from firewood cannot be measured in degrees, just as the nourishment from gardening is not measured merely in calories.

Now, the garden of the year is past. Lessons in the cold months ahead won't come from the fenced domain of the garden but from open, wooded hillsides of Goose Creek; from the splitting and stacking and stoking that will keep fires throwing flickers of flame through the glass door of the wood stove into this warm room from late September until mid-April. Then, as the days lengthen in the spring and the soil thaws through mud to crumbling dark loam once more, the garden's needs will become the focus of our labors. Ashes to ashes, dust to dust. And so it goes.

In these shorter days of autumn, as we move our energies from garden soil to open forest, we have come to a changing of the guard. Our garden is hibernating, and it is time to go hunt the bare bones of walnuts, locusts and oaks. It is hard work. It is good work. It is our economy, what we do, and in my ledger, there is no better pay for a day's work than this.

Vox Populi

The house was chilly when I got home—cooler inside than out. A somber October sun only a few shades paler than sky offered little light, and less heat. I stepped into my rubber boots—a country-dweller's slippers—for the short walk to the woodpile for an armload of kindling. A small fire through the glass doors of the woodstove would cheerify the dark afternoon, would take the edge off the damp-cold before Ann got home. Standing in a fine mist, I zipped up my jacket on the stone walkway outside the back door, and breathed in the familiar smell of mid-autumn's demise in a mulch of molding leaves. And then I heard it.

Truth is, the dog heard it first. His ears perked, suddenly alert. The unsettling commotion above us was not our repertoire of familiar country sounds; we put up our guard. It came from beyond the bare maples, from the near ridge behind the house.

From somewhere hidden in those young pine trees on the broken hillside came the anxious, ventriloquial voices of birds. Thousands of birds. Their angst filled the valley, louder even than the babble of the creeks. Grackles, probably, maybe mixed with other blackbird kin—the loathsome, hapless starlings. But I could see not a one of them. Their invisibility only added to the eeriness of their thousand opinions: Listen to me! I have an idea! Let's go that a'way! each one squeek-chirped to his incorporeal companions.

Rising, falling, they turned on their perches as each new spokesman, spokesbird, took the podium, a hundred giant rainsticks inverted over and over, tinkling waterdrop metallic voices that swelled just before they all took wing, became suddenly visible, followed the advice of the most insistent speaker; and they were gone from sight, then from sound only to rise and swirl and return to the same two trees out of hundreds of trees on the same ridge. Together, they vetoed their twentieth or twenty-first itinerary—undecided voters, uncertain of where or when, sure only that they must go, more or less south, more or less soon. And at once they flushed, and headed north.

Skywatch: The Leonids Meteor Shower

I left a warm bed, got dressed in every piece of clothing I could lift and carry, and stood outside in the dark for a half-hour this morning. With my neck craned, spinning slowly in circles, I waited in the cold to see the grand show of the Leonid Meteor Shower. My toes are still numb an hour later, and I need to find a good physical therapist to do some mobilization on my stiff sky-watcher's neck. Was it worth it? Yes indeed.

The light of a setting full moon and the wet haze in the predawn air washed out the weakest stars. But it was dark enough. In thirty minutes, I saw perhaps 200 meteors. Most were zips at the edge of vision. Some were spectacular, lighting up the valley in less than a blink, like a photographic flash. Others left persistent trails across the sky in the way an artist would lightly dash a perfectly straight line on black canvas with a luminescent pale blue pigment with a fine-tipped brush. One split into two, each fragment sizzling off to die dark death, extinguished in the protective shield of atmosphere.

"Give me a show!" I demanded for my efforts. Dazzle me with special effects. Entertain me. The predictable shower of stars fell, and on with the show. But before it, and after it, one spectator huddled against the cold of the dark side of the planet and knew moonlight and starlight, creek sounds and the stark silhouette of limbs against the heavens. These features do not come to indoor venues.

Will I make a habit of bundling up each morning to stand silent under a quiet sky where stars keep their places or not? No, I can't promise I will do this. But I have remembered again what night is like, and cold, and things moving out there beyond my vision and understanding. This, and another cup of hot coffee, is easily enough for me.

Ann's Falls

Our narrow valley is flanked by rugged hillsides overgrown in what mountain folk sometimes call a "laurel slick." These under-story shrub-forests of rhododendron and mountain laurel grow on steep and rocky grades where soil is thin and foot travel is nigh impossible. You'd be wise to find another way to get where you're going than to look for a path through such a place as this, but Ann was determined that this was just the way she would go.

Against the skyline along the crest on our east ridge, a gentle V-shaped cleft of sky marks where a wet-weather stream has cut its way down the mountainside, invisible beneath the arching greenery. For days after every hard rain, we leap over the little brook that swells out of this laurel thicket to flow across our footpath, bound eventually for the south fork of the Roanoke River. In the distance up the hillside we could hear—but could not see—that water was falling under the slick of dark, leathery leaves.

And here is what I must not forget: on her few days home the week after Christmas, in spite of all the to-do of the holidays, Ann was determined that she would reach that invisible waterfall. She would cut the twisted laurel and clear a trail up the steep slope to the little cataract. She would pull fallen limbs and debris from the shallow plunge pool beneath the rocky ledge. Finally, from two flat rocks and an old board she would fashion a seat where we—or she alone—could sit, sheltered from the pressure and hurry of the larger world. In her digging and tugging, in the clambering over the steep and secret place was such grand play, and we so seldom play any more.

But like the neglected trail she cleared through a laurel slick to tiny hidden falls, the memory of that brief window in time will soon be obscured by obligation and duty. Routine and the passage of anonymous and featureless days will shroud in forgetfulness the memory of that time—those special hours my wife spent purchasing her dream.

So that we can call up these images from the impenetrable thicket of the past, I will go back and add this page to our book of days, a way of remembering special hours too easily forgotten.

Where Are You From?

All who wander are not lost. ~ JRR Tolkien

When we are young, we live where we're born. For some of us, the place of our birth is a perfect fit and we never leave it. For others like me, something is missing there, and we look for home in places we have never been but long to find.

After college, my wife and I stayed in my birth state of Alabama just long enough to save a little money, have a baby and decide where it was that we belonged in this world. Somehow we knew then that home would be north of Alabama, and we understood that our lives were meant to be lived among mountains. When we found southwest Virginia in the mid-seventies, we felt we had come home. Or at least that we had found the larger neighborhood of round ridges and gentle valleys where some day, we would put down roots and stay. We have lived in or longed to return to Virginia ever since. And now, finally, we're here in Floyd County for good. But in all the world, I wonder: why here?

Something has drawn us here over the years, brought us back. A longing we cannot name has caused these hills to hold a nutrient we cannot live comfortably without. Maybe the force that has pulled us home could be called a persistent, inborn "sense of place". Others have used the term, defined it for themselves, found it—in the Far North, the Mid-West, the desert or shore. But what is it? Is it an essence in the air like the salmon sense as they migrate relentlessly back to the creeks where they were born? Is it a magnetic compatibility with geography, an imperceptible, persistent resonance in our bones that tells us that we are home? Or not?

"Where are you from?" a new acquaintance will ask.

It has been far easier to tell people where I live or have lived than to tell them where I am from. Unlike our grandparents who may have died in the same county where they were born, like many of my peers, I have followed careers wherever they might carry me, and "home" has pretty much been synonymous with our current mailing address. There has never been a family home place for me to go back to. How would I ever know when and where to settle down, to make roots for my children's children, to bond with a particular place for good?

It's odd how and when they happen—those flashes of insight that seem to be openings in the heavens, when light pours down into our own private darkness. When I had my revelation of belonging, it was though the words of Sharyn McCrumb, speaking at the Presbyterian Church in the tiny community of Floyd. I wondered if others felt the tremors I felt that night.

She described the serpentine rock under the Appalachian chain, the core of stone that binds the great backbone together. I perked up my ears: it begins just south of my home town in Alabama, she told us. From there, it stretches north underneath Floyd and all the way to Ireland. The image of this long unbroken line of history and stone conjured in my mind a map, and on it, I could see them in a perfect line: all of the towns I had chosen for homes in our wanderings.

I guess it just never occurred to me before that moment: in all of my seeming rootlessness, I have never lived far from the southern mountains. In my epiphany that night, I saw that I never could. The mountains held a gravity I could not escape; I had always been Appalachian. The mountains were my source, and I was a native son. And I knew then that I would come to feel more akin to others who claim this calling to place than to those who by accident of birth were born where I was born.

But what kind of allegiance does a native son owe these ridges and valleys? How much of who I am is because of where I've been called to live? Would I have become the same person had I been born on Midwestern prairie or Arctic tundra? How am I—how are we—shaped by the form and pulsing life and the history of these hills and this forest?

Whether we know or deny it, place molds into each of us its latitude and elevation, its geometry and chemistry. But it is possible to live so fast that we become oblivious to our relationship to the where of our lives. An intimate relationship with the land requires a daily attention to the particulars through every season.

What We Have Eyes to See

On an October drive across the northeast end of Floyd county, Ann and I took roads we'd traveled often when we lived near the parkway. Fallen leaves covered these once familiar twists and turns, and on this particular trip, for the first time, four small family cemetery plots stood out clearly against the deep blue of the fall sky. We are usually watchful for this kind of detail in the landscape, but neither one of us had ever noticed these old grave-yards on these roads and we wondered why that was.

As we drove, I retold the story of an old graveyard I found quite by accident many years ago. I was hiking alone in a remote Wythe County valley when I chanced upon the remains of a village. It had once bustled with human activity in farmhouses, barns and outbuildings now all but disappeared. Forest had reclaimed the clearings. Standing in the shade of what remained of an old stack-rock chimney, I tried to imagine what life must have been like there so long ago. On a knoll above me, a spreading oak of great size and age stood guard over the valley. I supposed it might have been growing there when this little community was young and thriving. I climbed the hill to get a closer look.

In its dappled shade among tall grasses, the old oak sheltered a dozen headstones. Each stood out of plumb, round-shouldered and crusted with gray-green lichens. Inscriptions of birth and death on the soft stone had worn away over the weathering decades.

When I first walked up on the neglected tombstones, it made me sad that they lay uncared for and abandoned. But by the time I lifted my pack and walked on, I had come to think that I would chose to be buried myself in just such an overgrown place as this with those I'd loved. In its dignified decay, this lost graveyard was fitting tribute to families who had cleared this forest, made their lives there, and now rested under oaks and broom sedge—ashes to ashes, forest to forest, they and their village had returned. When I'm gone, I'd prefer to be shrouded by brambles and lichen with my kin than to lie under polished marble in a manicured cemetery lawn, resting forever next to people I had never known.

Family burial plots speak to me of deep roots and a fixed history that I lack. And so I was surprised to discover that, for years, we'd driven past invisible cemeteries that suddenly now, our eyes could see clearly. Our vision hadn't changed; it's only that our perception is age-appropriate. A child looking out the window riding with us over that well-traveled stretch of road would have noticed all the swing sets and tree houses; a teenager would have paid attention to the fast cars or trucks parked behind the farm houses.

When we first moved to the county looking for a few acres and a house, what we saw clearly then were the realtors' signs. And now, it's the cemeteries that catch our attention—which is only right, I suppose. The days of tricycles, tree houses and hot trucks have passed. We've found our house and our home. And we know where we're moving next—down the road of time. We see that end more clearly every day. I realize now that life has a way of revealing its mysteries to our eyes only when the time is right for us to see them.

Calling Them By Name

On a clear, crisp afternoon in the first week in September, I spotted my first Monarch of the year over a meadow of goldenrod, boneset and milkweed. Some young folks were with me that day in the field along the New River Trail to see these creatures first hand, and to give them names for the first time. I held up, pointed out, and identified several dozen flowering plants and trees that afternoon. Afterwards one young lady asked if we might do this kind of hands-on outdoor study again. "This is the way I learn best" she said enthusiastically, a fact about herself it seemed she had only that hour discovered.

I had decided to take the group outdoors when I learned not a one of them could name a single wildflower in bloom in the nearest forest or pasture. These young people are not unusual in a generation that lacks names for things outdoors. They don't see deeply into nature, it seems, because they've not had much encouragement to look there. So many electronic and virtual distractions compete far too successfully for their attention. They have grown up in an era when our language in the digital world has grown rich while our vocabulary in the real world of nature has become sadly impoverished.

Beyond the vegetables and animal foods we purchase shrink-wrapped from the grocery store, many of us no longer can call our fellow creatures by name. The naming of things is often essential to our understanding of them and to our belonging among them, and there are costs to our ignorance. These young people who field-tripped with me are not sad in the way I am that the eastern hemlocks are dying, because they don't distinguish between a hemlock and any other kind of tree. Maybe it is significant that God set man the task of naming the creatures early on in Genesis as the first and necessary part of assuming our responsibility as stewards. What we have names for, we are more likely to notice and appreciate, less likely to ignore, abuse or consider of no consequence. We know our friends by name, and attend to them better than we do rank strangers. I wonder if we couldn't be better caretakers of the planet if we were on a first name basis with more of its inhabitants, and knew more about their families and their kin.

But should they care to, can a parent, a teacher or a newly-enlightened field trip student reclaim the names of the things forgotten and ignored? Can we learn our way around the meadow or forest where our children are so sadly out of touch? Yes, I think we can: by nurturing intentional vision.

Go slowly in nature and stop often. Look for the particulars. You might even take notes and draw sketches. Learn a dozen trees and recognize them in leaf, fruit and branch in every season. Learn a dozen wildflowers from spring, from summer and from autumn. And rekindle curiosity and wonder. Each insect or flower holds its own mystery and unique design. Be able to name a dozen birds, first by sight, then by their call alone. Know some salamanders—while they last—and a few dragonflies and even some common spiders and snakes.

Then, teach your children to see more deeply as you have done. On regular walks around your back yard, pasture or woods show them your own care for detail and watch how quickly they come to see the small world at their feet and give names to its creatures. Pick twigs from plants like spicebush, sassafras, and teaberry; scratch and sniff them and resurrect the neglected sense of smell that so powerfully builds memories in the out-of-doors. Turn rocks, and pluck blooms (not entire plants.) Use a hand lens to see more detail.

And after seeing, find the names for the things you see. This has never been easier to do. The computer is a quick and convenient tool for this, but my first advice would be to build a library of field guides you can carry with you and hold in your hands over the years. Study what you have found while sitting in the grass under the trees and ask for help from your children. Even the smallest can compare pictures.

Never before has the natural world needed each of us to know it, care for it and act on its behalf in such a way as it does in our times. We cannot be responsible stewards of a threatened planet if its creatures are distant, anonymous and irrelevant strangers. Be more aware than you've ever been in this cathedral made without hands, as John Muir called our world. Make friends of its inhabitants and call them by name.

Home and Hearth

Our move from Alabama to Virginia in 1975 introduced us to real winter, and our southern bones were not at all prepared for it. That first season of snow and ice, my young family had to hug the cast iron radiators to stay warm. We knew early on that there must be a better way to keep from freezing indoors. We bought our first wood-stove for reasons of sheer survival.

The day they delivered our Fisher Momma Bear stove, I thought we'd conquered winter's cold at last. But to feed our cast-iron heater, we owned neither truck nor chain-saw. With Ann on push and me on pull, we bow-sawed our wood from deadfall by permit from the National Forest. We hauled it home in a Datsun hatchback, full down on its rear shocks, and split it piece by gnarly piece with an axe. This was the famous wood you've heard about that heats you twice (or more.) For a naïve immigrant, the energy that goes into wood heat was a shocking lesson in "simple living." Other lessons learned by the novice country mice that year included creosote. And flue fires. But those are stories for another time.

As we grew into our new southwest Virginia lifestyle and became comfortable with the rhythms of the heating year, I began to appreciate that hearth and home are words that do truly belong together. When the cold winds whistled over the roof and the windows glazed with ice, family life was centered around that black box with the kettle perking on top. The kids sprawled on the floor beside it and played dominoes. Ann sat in the high-backed chair with cross-stitch in her lap while I read or played the guitar in the warmth of wood we'd gathered from our own hillsides.

Thirty years and a hundred cords of hardwood later, I still enjoy the heat of wood, but I'm not quite as energetic now about the gathering of it, or the splitting, or stacking, or toting as I once was. The ground, it seems, gets a bit farther away from my hands with every passing year, and I swear a cord of wood didn't used to be so doggone heavy. But we'll hold out against the temptation of alternatives, especially now that other forms of heat are so expensive and might not be consistently reliable through life's storms to come.

The trees will continue to die and fall in our little valley, and it seems wasteful to give away such a windfall of energy to the decomposers on the forest floor. I'll be obliged by habit and my frugal nature to bring in the wood for yet another winter to feed this iron pet that lives with us. But there are purposes other than warmth to burn wood. I know this will sound strange, but the woodstove does seem like a family member, and it wouldn't be Virginia winter without it in our home.

The stove's care and feeding for the next six months will be as essential as our own eating and breathing. We will open its mouth and feed it often; we will check its temperature to make sure it becomes neither too hot nor too cold and we'll watch its breath out the chimney for signs of congestion. After feedings we will clean up the crumbs with a small brush and a dustpan. All winter long, we will pay homage with split oak, locust and ash—offerings to this revered, cast iron symbiotic creature in our midst.

From these first brisk, gray fall days until the crocus and bloodroot pop up in the sunshine of April, the stove will be the first thing we care for each morning, the last duty we attend to every winter night. Before bedtime, we will sit in our chairs and watch the flames leap behind the glass door of the stove, and nod in the drowsy glow. From our bed in the dark, we'll hear it purring contentedly in ticks and pops as it warms, and we will fall asleep in its flickering light.

Where I am Married

I can't say yet that I understand fully how one feels or follows a "sense of place." I do know that, for me, this siren call toward home has come from the southern Appalachians. All of the places I've chosen to live my adult life have been in or within sight of the mountains. It is a kind of marriage, perhaps.

A man can be fond of women, but he will settle down in a relationship and build a love affair full of meaning with one woman. And so it is, ultimately—if we are fortunate—with finding our place. I am drawn to the Southern Highlands. I have a particularly strong love for the Blue Ridges of these ancient Appalachians. But I sleep every night in this singular configuration of creek and forest and high ridge that I now call home. For the first time in my life, I feel a monogamous fidelity to one fixed and particular place that is as deep and permanent a commitment as the vows I have taken to this one woman, my wife.

In these few years of growing close to a place that has become our home, I have had the blessing of time alone here, and we have consummated our bonds, this land and I: on slow winter walks along Nameless Creek; in quiet summer mornings standing on the front porch with my coffee; during autumn afternoons alone on the ridge sitting with my back against the smooth trunk of a tulip poplar watching pasture grasses down below swirl in the wind like coursing, surging wildebeests on the Serengeti.

It has not always been an easy companionship. I confess that I have resented being here at times—the sameness, the separation, the hardships of living faithfully committed to this bucolic enclave week after week. But the relationship still grows. The more I come to know the shape and moods of this valley through the seasons, the more I know myself as I walk its paths, photograph and write of its beauties and imbibe its wonders every day. And the more I know that we can live together— 'til death do us part.

Bend in the Road

Hard frost last night. Sky is pinking up. The reflection of the woodstove flames dance orange against the windowpane, framing an utter calm, cold landscape beyond the glass. The barn roof is white, the butterfly bush outside my window limp with ice crystals fringing every curled and faded leaf.

How womblike—the warmth of the stove, the familiar touch of chair and desk, this old flannel shirt I wear as if it were my birth skin. I love this place, so constant, so fully known and at hand. This place: this room, this house, this valley, these mountains, this time in our lives. Especially now, as winter creeps closer and the days grow short, I appreciate the roof overhead, the full stacks of firewood, the canning in the basement and slow moments like this to see our blessings, the ordinary that we too often take for granted.

We can't know what's coming around the bend in the road. But it has been a very nice road, that's for sure.

About the Author

Fred is a lifelong biology watcher, photographer and teacher, with MS degrees in vertebrate zoology and physical therapy. In 2002, Fred temporarily left his former professions and began to write from his home in the remote corner of a rural Virginia county that needs only one traffic light. Since then, he has recorded more than a dozen essays for broadcast on the Roanoke NPR station, WVTF. He writes a biweekly column called *The Road Less Traveled* for the Floyd Press; and he has pieces published in journals and magazines including Birmingham Arts Journal, Greenprints, Pet Life, Flow, Blue Ridge Country Magazine and Nantahala Review. He credits his weblog, *Fragments from Floyd*, for the discipline of daily writing—the story that has now become this book.

After a brief time away during which writing was his focus, Fred has returned to teaching biology at Radford University and to physical therapy practice in a nearby clinic. When he isn't teaching, treating patients or writing, he enjoys gardening, natural history, digital photography and—as long as his joints lasts—gathering the firewood to heat their restored farm house on Goose Creek. Fred and Ann have two grown children, one grandchild, and always at least one Labrador retriever.